LEAP!

A Journey to Personal Power and Possibility

Jonathan Creaghan's latest book: a humorous and striking fictional journey that, unlike usual self-help books full of psychological Jargon, is an activation button that awakens the desires within the reader to move forward with their own lives. *"You've never read a book like this, but you will recognize the story."*

"A wonderfully original book that will inspire your best life."

—**Robin Sharma**
Best selling author of
The Monk Who Sold His Ferrari

"We all have chasms to leap when on our journey through life. Jonathan's book gives us the tools to travel through life and face challenges with clarity."

—**Rick Spencer**
President, SPENCER STEEL

"It was something I could read in a day and let it cook!"

—**Angela Hoyt**
CEO, EVOLUTION GROUP INC.

"A great read—I connected with the characters. In fact, everyone will connect with the characters on some level!"

—**Trevor Bond**
Partner, Financial Planner
LONDON WEALTH MANAGEMENT GROUP

"Believe and succeed. Jonathan Creaghan, author of *Leap!* breaks down the internal barrier and opens your mind to endless personal growth and prosperity, but you must act now!"

—Donald Brunette
Vice President, Sales & Marketing
ENVIROTECH OFFICE SYSTEMS

"A powerful tool for change."

—Lori Hisson
Inspiring Speakers

"While reading the note on page 73, somewhere between Detroit and Denver, I experienced a calmness regarding my current state and realized the control I really have over it."

—Jim Juniper
Entrepreneur

"*Leap!* will take you from where you are, back to where you were, so you can find out where you are going. A truly enlightening and inspirational book."

—John McKenzie
President
MCKENZIE'S ASSOCIATED AUCTIONEERS

"A brilliant mind created this book. It should be read by those who are and are not yet ready to take a *Leap!* The insight and wisdom presented will shift your outlook in life."

Principal Designer
NMC GROUP

LEAP!

A Journey to Personal Power and Possibility

Jonathan Creaghan

The J.D. Creaghan Group

2003

www.leapsafely.com

Canadian Cataloguing in Publication Data

Creaghan, Jonathan, 1960-
        Leap! a journey to personal power and possibility

ISBN 0-9686432-1-3

1. Self-actualization (Self-help). I. J. D. Creaghan Group. II. Title.

BF637.S4C 74 1999   158.1   C99-932966-9

Cover designed by Natalie M. Cooper & Mosaic Design Inc.
Designed by Fortunato Design, Toronto
Edited by Oakwell Boulton, Toronto
Printed and Bound in Canada by Webcom Limited, Toronto

To my boys Spencer and Aidan.
May your lives be filled with
challenge and excitement.

Acknowledgements

Leap! only came to life with the support of friends and family. There are many people who have played a direct role in the life of the project and many more who do not even know they have influenced its success. Thank you all.

First and foremost my wife Joanne, whose belief in *Leap!* has been unfailing even when we wondered if it would ever get out of the computer.

To John Christensen, Joe Gaetan, and Roy Saunderson, who saw a vision for *Leap!* much larger than my own. Your constant energy and challenging has been much appreciated.

Dharma Gaynes, who saw within the original transcript messages and ideas that became translated into the storytelling experiences. Your assistance has been invaluable.

Ed Seduikis, your enthusiasm for the book is appreciated. Thanks.

To my father Tom, thank you for your continued support and insights.

My mother Nan, your undying desire to help the less fortunate has played an important role in my own life.

The team who helped put the book together, especially my assistant Carol Longworth and program director, Natalie Cooper.

Finally I would like to thank all of my clients past and present. Your personal leaps are truly inspiring.

Contents

Contents

Introduction

I began writing *Leap!* as a tool to assist others in coping with the chaotic and insecure times we find ourselves immersed in. But as I continued writing, it was clear that the story was really about living with greater freedom, passion and influence in this chaotic world. Where we are able to uncover our power and tap into our potential to create the lives we have always wanted to have, the increasing awareness of which allows us to live with a deep sense of inner peace, elegance and trust.

I sat down to write only when I was able to articulate the universal patterns of thought and behavior I had seen in my clients or when I had made a personal discovery. Duxter, the hero in the story, continued on his journey while I continued on mine. There were many times throughout the book when what I wrote had a significant impact on how I should proceed in my own life. It would have been so much easier had I sat down and read a dozen or so books on transformation and then regurgitated my knowledge onto paper. But for me, the story is straight from the hearts of those people who have taken a leap in their own lives.

Duxter is an 'every person'. No matter how successful one is, we all share in his dilemma and self-doubt when we pursue possibility at the highest level. We are Duxter because to pursue possibility is to go to the edge of our comfort zone and leap over into unknown territory. Yet, it is when we do this, that we are most fully alive and present in our own life.

It is said that most people live their lives somewhere between boredom and apathy. Certainly, this was where Duxter lived and where I lived until I became aware of my own journey. We go about our daily lives oblivious of our surroundings and the persistent "niggle" that every once in a while tells us things are not quite right. This "niggle" can go on for years or a short time. Sometimes the "niggle" must scream at us before we hear it; like when we experience some kind of life crisis: job loss, sickness, divorce, and bankruptcy. Sometimes the "niggle" is more subtle. We just wake up one day and decide it is time to grow.

Yet there is an important distinction to make that is crucial. That is, are we living a reactive life where we continually make decisions in reaction to a past or present force or occurrence? Or are we seeking to live a creative and masterful life where we choose to act toward a goal or possibility? To live a masterful life means that no matter what positive or negative event one experiences, we have the personal power and confidence to use our circumstances as an opportunity to forward our goals and dreams. In a nutshell, this is the transformation Duxter makes. By the end of the book, he is at peace.

This story has been written to evoke thought and contemplation; to provide you, the reader, with an opportunity to reflect upon your own possibility of a joyous and complete life and the leap required to attain it. Throughout, there will be questions and statements that are designed not only to provoke an answer from our hero, but from you the reader as well. Ask yourself the questions. Think about your answers.

Introduction

Of course, we are all ultimately and individually responsible for ourselves and I ask the questions of Duxter as I ask them of you, based on answers that are meaningful and important, answers that create the motivation and opportunity you need.

This is a short book and so you are free to finish it as quickly as you choose or to take your time. You may also let it skim over you, or you may let those parts that you recognize and to which you relate evoke a reaction. Be aware of that reaction, it is trying to tell you something and let the words sink in.

Jonathan Creaghan

PART 1
Present Focus – Present Action

"A state of being in which a person's energy is directed to the way things are NOW. He or she will make decisions and live in reactions to activities or occurrences as they happen, with no serious thought of their implications for the future. Typically, dreams and goals are unformulated, have been forgotten, or are suppressed."

Duxter's Companion

Nothing Happens… for a While

Duxter Hexter rolled out of bed for the sixteen thousand, four hundred and twenty-fifth time in his life. His feet hit the floor and he moaned as his niggle made its presence known to him again. He was forty-five years of age and this was like any other day. Prepare for work, have breakfast, catch the downtown bus into the office and be in his chair by eight a.m. He didn't really have an office. He had a desk in a cubicle in the middle of a large floor, surrounded by twenty other workstations.

Duxter wasn't unhappy, although he wasn't exactly happy either. If he were to try to explain it, there was a gnawing in his stomach, a little niggle way in the back recesses of his mind, that kept on reminding him all was not quite right. He looked down at the pile of folders in front of him and sighed. If only it were the way it used to be. It was friendlier, more relaxed, when everyone knew the job was for life. It was easy to focus on doing the job well, back then, he mumbled to himself. That was how he felt, deep down inside, but then he told himself those days were gone forever.

Just for example, yesterday he had an e-mail from on high saying that he could expect many changes over the next few years. When was this going to end? The last changes didn't work out and he was still paying the price by having more responsibility, and working longer hours, for only marginally better pay. He thought himself lucky though, because he still had his job while many of his friends had gone through several over the past few years.

Duxter was good at his job. He made sure of that. He

managed the customer service department. Twenty staff worked under him. In total his department, one of five spread around the world, serviced the needs of many thousands of customers. Handling their complaints, and making any changes that were required to ensure they were satisfied. For the first year it had been challenging, but after that he got to be so good at it that he didn't really have to think too hard. Now he was being told to upgrade his skills and knowledge yet again. Not that this was bad in itself, but the real issue for him was knowing that whether he did the job well or not he wouldn't influence the world one bit. Deep down inside, if he was truly honest with himself, he had to admit that he was restless, incomplete and empty.

"I have a family, adult responsibilities, no time, less money, and more pressure," he would gladly tell anyone who would listen.

Oh, yes… he thought of leaving, but for all his complaints the pay was OK and the benefits were good. He had four weeks holiday a year and a good pension building up. What else was there to ask? His father and mother had always told him to stay with the Firm. "Make yourself indispensable," they would say. "Then the Firm will look after you!" He had always been told that Security was the main thing. "Who really likes their job anyway?" Now, of course, security was out the window and it seemed that everyone was dispensable. Well, in any case, he thought to himself smugly, the Company needed him. He was a "Specialist." Without him, the department would break down.

By midmorning his routine was well under way and his day was going like any other. Handle the more serious complaints, go to meetings, check the information against standards and policy. But then, as he sat at his desk, looking around at his staff going off for their coffee break, Duxter

Hexter's mind drifted back to a conversation with a stranger he had met at the last year's Christmas party.

Duxter had confided to this total stranger that in truth he would rather be someplace else than where he was. Maybe running his own little store, or teaching kids, or doing something with more personal meaning. There were so many things he had yet to accomplish. Maybe learning to fly a plane or writing childrens' books. He enjoyed creating bedtime stories for his kids when they were younger. "This job," said Duxter, "wasn't what life was all about." Surely he hadn't been born to do this job? And he said all of this to someone he'd never seen around the office before.

He recalled the unexpected question he was asked, the question that had been niggling at him now for almost a year. It was simply this:

"What is preventing you from making the change?"

The question seemed innocent enough. Duxter even thought it was rather a good question. But he remembered his feeling of panic. The wish to run away, rather than give an answer.

"Well... I... I mean... I mean *I can't*," said Duxter. "You know you can't always have what you want, I mean there are some things you just have to accept as not being possible. So I'm not totally happy here, but the pension's good, and anyway... anyway, ... I mean... I have obligations, you know, like bills to pay and a family to care for."

"How do you know your family would not want you to make a change, if they knew it was in their best long term interest?"

Again the feeling of being cornered... Of course he had never discussed the idea. He had always assumed they wouldn't like it. But he'd never asked them. "Oh, I *know* them," he replied. "They wouldn't want me to make a change. It would be too disruptive." He was anxious to end this uncomfortable conversation with this inquisitive stranger.

"Too disruptive for whom?"

The stranger did not blink or move. This was a direct challenge. An uneasy silence filled the space between them. Duxter started to shuffle. He tried to excuse himself but he could not move. It was almost like he was welded to the spot, not really ready for a challenge but unable to prevent one from coming.

"Well, you know… I mean… I just bought a new car and… well, it would be difficult, that's all." A smile froze on his face but his eyes revealed something of which he was not wholly aware. He was afraid of changing his life. He looked down as he spoke. He really wanted to leave, to go anywhere, rather than stay where he was. This stranger was like a dog, unwilling to concede that the game of tag was over.

"Duxter!" Duxter looked around for the source of the voice. A sigh of relief unwittingly passed through him, but it was Smith.

"I haven't seen you for a while, Duxter! How are you doing?"

He shook Smith's hand and was about to introduce him to the stranger but the spell was broken and the stranger was gone.

"Well," chirped Smith, "how's the job up on eighth? Still the same old stuff as always? Still doing the same thing? What's it been now, ten, twelve years?"

Duxter's eyes looked away as he answered affirmative to every question. He hated bumping into Smith. It was always the same. Smith was going places, and had to rub it in that he, Duxter, was still in the same department.

Smith had started in Duxter's department five years before and had since moved on to a respectable position in upper middle management, leaving Duxter behind. Meeting Smith was the last thing Duxter would have wanted at that moment, if it had not been for the stranger.

"Well... so..." Duxter hesitated. He knew he shouldn't ask but couldn't stop himself. He was being dragged down by a dangerous undertow. It was too late, he felt the tug of the current as he opened his mouth. He already knew the answer, but out came the question anyway. It was like he wanted to drown himself in the answer. "So, are you still Manager of Inventory Services?"

Whoosh,—under he went.

"No, I just got a promotion to oversee the whole area. In fact, you're working for me now, buddy boy," said Smith, slapping Duxter on the back and laughing.

Down and down went Duxter, as the slap pushed him farther into the depths. He looked up and saw the surface of the water from underneath, the rays of the sun penetrating the surface that was so far out of his reach. He felt the current dragging him further into darkness.

"How...wonderful!" Duxter said, struggling to touch the rays just below the surface.

"Hey, I have to run now," said Smith. "I see Olivia over at the punch bowl. Hey, buddy boy, we'll talk." He pointed his finger and clicked his tongue as he smiled. He was gone before Duxter had a chance to reply.

Then Duxter crashed to the surface, like a whale come from the depths of the ocean to gather more air in its lungs.

And now Duxter was back at his desk. The sight of the papers, the feel of the keyboard under his hands and the knowledge that he was safe again made him laugh.

He read the newspaper on the way home as he always did. He particularly enjoyed the travel section, all those exotic places. He was longing to get away, to start anew. Tahiti, Tobago, Africa, Spain, Europe, anywhere. He was scanning page four of his favourite section where tucked away at the bottom right hand corner his eyes caught a very strangely worded paragraph that would change his life forever:

DON'T READ THIS PARAGRAPH IF YOU ARE HAPPY, SATISFIED AND GOING SOMEWHERE

We are a new travel company in town, specializing in personal tours. You create your own travel plans. Explore places you may not have been to in a while - exotic, wild lands - at your own pace! Call 1-888-Duxcall for further information. *That includes you Duxter Hexter!*

There at the bottom of the ad was his name. How the...! He couldn't believe it. Duxter slammed the paper shut and looked around the bus, hoping no one had seen his reaction. No one had. He cautiously opened the paper again and stared at the ad in disbelief. What Duxter did not know was that only he could see his name. Anyone else who read the ad, if they saw it at all, saw only his or her own name. The message was intended for anyone who was feeling incomplete. It was seen by 76.3 % of the population.

It was sent through the newspapers, radio and television.

It was written on sidewalks, on traffic signs, on billboards, on desks. Wherever people went or worked, played, sat, read, or whatever they did, they would see it. And it wasn't restricted to age, size, beauty, success, failure, wealth, race, colour, religion, or anything else. It went out to anyone who, at that particular time, was feeling empty. And so it came to Duxter. He wasn't really happy. He just didn't know it yet.

No one was home when he arrived. His wife must be working late and the kids were away at an overnight school function. Duxter headed for the phone. He didn't know why it was important, it was like an overwhelming need to do as the ad said. He knew he was happy some of the time. Who didn't have problems? Who was going somewhere all of the time?

His finger dialled the number anyway.

Two days later a letter arrived on his doorstep. He opened it with much anticipation and anxiety. Inside was a single sheet of paper, that read as follows:

Dear Sir/Madam,

Congratulations on choosing to make your travel arrangements through us. We look forward to meeting with you in the near future and have reserved a room for you at one of our luxurious hotels. See you at your earliest convenience.

You will note, on the back of this page, a ticket. To begin your "Personal Tours" please insert it in the automatic teller machine at your corner milk store.

Sincerely,

I. M. Can't

Later that evening, Duxter went to the corner milk store

and inserted the ticket into the machine and waited and waited and waited. Nothing happened. He waited some more and still nothing happened. He left the store feeling dejected.

In fact, nothing happened for days.

It was not too long before he fell back into his old routine. The anticipation of waiting for the unexpected left him. The nervous excitement of taking a risk disappeared. He felt embarrassed and silly for having been sucked in by a stupid call to action.

Duxter Finally Understands

He came home one day and found a letter from the travel company. He opened it with some trepidation.

Dear Mr Hexter:,
I trust your travels are going well. By now you have probably realized that you have gone Nowhere. As our ad described, you create your own travel plans. You have decided to go Nowhere and we commend you on your decision. I trust you will enjoy your stay.
Sincerely,

I. M. Can't

"Nowhere! I am not nowhere! I am here at home! Waiting for something to happen, a brochure to arrive, anything."

Little did Duxter realize that he was, in fact, travelling. He was touring around a very small confined world, whose boundaries consisted of his house, his work, and most importantly his own limiting beliefs about what was possible. Duxter was very sad. He sat in front of the T.V. flipping channels. He went to bed that night feeling very sorry for himself.

That night Duxter tossed and turned. He woke up several times because his niggle was getting louder. He recalled the letter "...you have probably realized you have gone nowhere... we commend you on your decision." The niggle wouldn't stop. He paced the floor faster. "Nowhere" he heard himself say "...You create your own travel plans..." Could it be true? He was finally able to find his way back to his bed, but only because he was too tired to fight the niggle any longer.

The next morning, he woke up with a start and sat bolt upright in bed. With utter clarity he realized that he WAS actually going nowhere. Just like the letter had indicated. He had been travelling for years and not knowing it. The distant markings of his future had disappeared, his destination unknown. He had forgotten where he was going.

Now, as anyone who has ever been Nowhere can tell you, Nowhere is as unrecognizable as anywhere until you realize you are there. Nowhere is bleak indeed. The land is flat and barren, there are no apparent markings to help you guide yourself out. Once thriving forests are shriveled sticks, rivers are dried up cesspools. It is dry, sandy, and dead. Anything that was alive is now half covered by the endlessly shifting sands that seem to overtake all but the strongest of creatures. But even the strongest sit around all day waiting for things to happen to them and for them. And Duxter had been waiting around for things to happen.

Unless you are aware of the approaching signs, you can find yourself in Nowhere without warning because it has no boundaries. It usually begins with an expectation that someone will help you.

It had crept up on Duxter slowly, quietly, dangerously. Now it was upon him. Years of ignoring his true desires, of playing it safe, of staying at his job for the holidays and the benefits, not for the challenges or enjoyment of the work. Unaware that his behaviour was really sending him a coded message, he had never bothered to sit down and decipher it. It had taken years to creep up on him, but it took only an instant to shock his mind into awareness.

That morning, after waiting aimlessly for what seemed to be days, Duxter finally realized where he was. He was indeed Nowhere.

Now you may feel that Duxter was hopelessly lost. However, the truth of the matter is that on realizing he was going Nowhere he was in fact well on his way to going Somewhere. At least now, he had a free choice... to decide to stay Nowhere or to go Someplace else. As far as Duxter knew that choice had not existed before.

Fortunately, Duxter finally knew he was Nowhere and he wanted to go anywhere but there. He jumped out of bed, quickly dressed, and headed for the door in a panic. He opened the door in a rush, took a step and fell into space. The stairs were gone. He was falling through emptiness. "HEYYY!!!" He was falling and should have been terrified, but he wasn't. It was more a feeling of surprise and confusion. He fell farther and farther and kept on falling...

Going Nowhere Fast

Duxter landed on a sand dune with a thud. It was like he dropped out of the sky, as a bird might drop from the nest when learning to fly.

He picked himself up from the ground and dusted himself off. He was slightly dazed and very confused.

"Hey, you! Hey, you over there!"

The voice slowly seeped into Duxters' consciousness. He looked around and noticed a person getting out of a truck, walking toward him. The tall, dusty, thin man was dressed in khakis, a wide-brimmed hat and heavy leather boots.

"Hey, you!"

Duxter pointed to his own chest, quizzically. "Who me?"

"Ya, you. Do you see anyone else around here in this Godforsaken place?"

"No, but..."

"Look, you going to get in the truck or just stand there in this blazing sun? I got another pick-up to make. There seems to be more and more of you out here these days."

"I don't even know you..."

"Ya, well I don't know you either. You could be some sort of crackpot or something. All I know is we got a call from head office to expect someone to drop in. I was told to pick you up and transport you to the outpost. That's all I was told. So, are you coming or not?"

"Well, I suppose if I must. I don't see any other options." Duxter jumped into the truck and they started off.

"Ya, that's the funny thing about this place."

"What are you talking about?" demanded Duxter.

"A lack of options — in Nowhere I mean. When you're going nowhere it's difficult to see options at all. That's one of the things that's obvious, living here. It's like it's in the air or something... I don't know."

Duxter fell silent. He looked out the window at the barren, dry landscape. His mind was filled with thoughts and questions. He noticed a license hanging from the rear view mirror:

Jake (Rims) LeBarge
Officer #06345

Duxter looked over at the driver. Who was this guy? He read further:

L.S.R.U.

Lost Soul Recovery Unit
Western Frontier Outpost Team

L...S...R...U... he said to himself, pondering the meaning of the letters. Duxter was about to ask Jake to explain his license when he saw a small building up ahead.

It was a small, barnboard building, maybe twenty feet by twenty feet, with a large, overhanging verandah. It was raised on stilts, maybe two feet off the desert floor. Duxter noticed a small, upright building off to the left. "That couldn't be what I think it is, could it?" His eyes went back to the main building. A sign was nailed to the roof.

The hand painted quote was too long for the sign. Whoever wrote it had to squish in the last few words.

What kind of place is this? They can't even design a sign and they're going to outfit me! Duxter was indignant.

The truck skidded to a stop.

"O.K. This is as far as I take you. Good luck."

Duxter jumped out of the truck. "But…" before Duxter could say anything in protest, Jake roared off. The dust from the wheels covered Duxter with a thin coating.

Just what was going on here? Duxter was getting frustrated now. No explanations, no courtesy. Silence filled the air. The whole area seemed deserted. Duxter walked into the building, the screen door slamming behind him.

"So, you finally made it." Duxter came face to face with a tired looking old man who had spent too much time in the sun. His skin was tough but his eyes were sharp. He was holding a knapsack in his right hand. Here was a man who could help, thought Duxter.

"I hope Jake wasn't too hard on you," said the old man. "He's not really a bad fella once you get to know him. Myself, I'm Bart. Pleased ta meet ya."

Duxter shook his hand. "Look, I don't know who you are, but if there's a phone I could use, I could call my wife and…"

"Nope. No phone here," interrupted Bart. "No need for one."

Duxter was shocked. "What do you mean, 'no need'? Of course there is. How do you order supplies? What if there was an accident? What if...?"

"Never been no accident. Jake's here a couple times a week. No need for a phone."—There was a pause. Duxter's eyes widened at the possibility of a wayback.

"Good, so I could get a ride back with Jake?"

"Now hold on. Don't reckon that's possible. Don't want you hanging around here for two days disturbin' my peace, blitherin' on about your problems. Nope, my job's to give you this here knapsack and send you on your way." Bart reached out to hand him the knapsack.

"That's it?" Duxter said, grabbing the knapsack from Bart. "Just this knapsack? What about food, clothing, a map, a flashlight? What kind of place is this? Come on, you gotta help me!"

"Well..." Bart paused. He seemed lost in his own thoughts.

"What?" Duxter yelled. "What do you have to tell me?"

"Well, it seems to me this here bag came with some kinda' pamphlet. Let me go into the back and rustle it up."

"A pamphlet, oh great! How is that going to help?"

Bart sauntered off, mumbling something about a long lost box.

Duxter sat down, sighing. "Oh, man. What am I doing here? There must be a way to get back home." Duxter looked around. The shelf-lined walls were filled with tin cans, stacked blankets, and dry goods. Fry pans were hanging from wire hooks, a canoe was hanging from the ceiling. What the heck was a canoe doing here? There wasn't water to be found for miles. He'd had enough. He would take control of this crazy place. If they weren't going to help him, he would help himself. He now had a knapsack. He'd fill it up with food and water and get on his way. This place was truly outrageous.

"Look, I'll just help myself to some of the food here and be on my way," he yelled, hoping Bart would respond. He walked over to the canned goods. "Hmmm. Let's see, yes, beans, stew, spaghetti. I'll also need water and…." He reached for the cans. They wouldn't budge. No matter how hard he pulled they wouldn't come off the shelf.

"Ahhhgh… What is going on?"

"Ehhh…? D'ya say something?" Bart came back with the information. "I'm sure now, I told ya all ya get is the knapsack," responding to Duxters' attempt at retrieving the cans.

"Well, yes, but…." He moved away from the shelf.

"Look, sit down and cool off a spell." Bart pushed Duxter into a chair. "The sign says you will get exactly what you need. That's it, nothing more."

"You got to be kidding. I just thought you made it up to be cute. I didn't know you meant it."

"I don't say nothin' I don't mean," responded Bart.

Duxter took a deep breath and slowed himself down. "So what do I do now?"

"You take the knapsack and be on your way. It's no more complicated than that. Everyone is always complicatin' things more than they need be."

"You aren't very helpful," responded Duxter.

Bart laughed, showing a gap in his teeth. "Hee, hee. Seems to me that depends on how you look at it, now doesn't it son. Now, listen up. I gotta go clean up the mess I made lookin' for this here booklet. You read it over. If you have any questions, I can't say I'll be of much help." Duxter took the brightly coloured tag describing the knapsack:

To the wearer of this bag

"This
exquisite, yet hardy
bag will change the way you
travel forever. The sense of adventure
and the desire to push forward and
perform are analogous to the message this
bag conveys when you put it over your
shoulder. This bag represents the sum of
who you are and who you want to be in
life. This bag is the genuine article.
There is no other bag exactly
like it anywhere."

Hmmm, Duxter was intrigued. What kind of bag can promise all that? He read on…

- *Roomy design for easy accessibility*
- *Comes complete with all you'll ever need to know*
- *Guaranteed for all the lifetimes you will ever have*
- *A timeless design that gets better with age*
- *Space enough to store universal truths*

Features

✔ *genuine cowhide*
✔ *leather drawstring closure with flap overlid*
✔ *two roomy, buckled and gussetted pockets*
✔ *padded shoulder straps*
✔ *hand grip*
✔ *superior construction and quality*

For the first time since he'd held it, Duxter looked closely at the knapsack. The size was perfect, neither too large nor too small, nor too heavy nor too light. The leather was extraordinarily soft to the touch. It had beautiful buckles, and padded shoulder straps. How would he describe the colour... tan? Except that when he opened the pockets, he could see the real colour was almost a cream tone. It was changing colours with age. It was growing a deeper, richer shade of its original colour. He opened it up and looked inside. He drew in his breath at what he saw sitting on the bottom. Huuuuhhhh, how can that be?

"I'm not sure if you're interested in this," interrupted Bart, holding a piece of paper.

Duxter looked up from the bag as if he had seen a miracle. "What? I'm sorry, I didn't hear what you said."

"I found this sitting on the floor. It looks like instructions or something."

"Here, let me see that." Duxter almost jumped off the chair. Running over, he grabbed the paper from Bart's hands.

Please note, the following information is very important:

*"This bag was custom made for only one traveller. It cannot be traded, or exchanged for another model. It is priceless, nothing has a comparable value. It cannot be given away. It is the sole property of the wearer. Once put on, it can never leave the awareness of the wearer. **It is not machine washable**.*

Before using please follow these printed instructions:

1. *Please print your name on the space provided on the inner side of the flap.* Duxter did as requested.

2. *Before wearing, make sure all the stuffing has been removed.* Duxter had already looked inside and seen none.

3. Do not place glass containers that may break or explode in the bag.

"Ya, ya," exclaimed Duxter impatiently. "That's not what I'm looking for." He read on.

*4. Though other items can be stored in it, to fully exploit its potential please store only experiences in it. The manufacturer advises you to **take only from the past what you need to get to the future**. Leave all else behind. This will ensure that the integrity of the knapsack is maintained throughout your journey.*

"Yes, now we are getting somewhere," thought Duxter.

5. The contents of this knapsack have been carefully selected for their usefulness to the wearer and may have little relevance to someone else.

A packing checklist has been provided:

❑ Learnings	❑ Information
❑ Memories	❑ Successes
❑ Knowledge	❑ Experiences
❑ Skills	❑ Openness
❑ Values	❑ Strengths
❑ Observations	❑ Self awareness
❑ Possibility	❑ Wisdom
❑ Truth	❑ Knowingness
❑ Trust	❑ Insights
❑ Future Vision	❑ Free Will

"Amazing, simply amazing," Duxter laughed. He went back to the knapsack and reached inside and brought forth a memory just as the packing check-list had outlined. As he peered at it more closely, he confirmed what he thought he had seen earlier. There he was as a child sitting on his father's knee. He saw his father laugh, he heard himself giggle with delight as he went bounding into the air. True joy suffused his face.

"Oh my God, how can this be?"

"I don't know what you are talking about," said Bart. "The bag is empty."

"No… No it isn't. It is filled with everything I need. You were right all along. Thank you, thank you." He leapt up to shake Bart's hand. "Look, I guess I better get going. I've taken up too much of your time already."

"I'll say!—I was worried I'd have to feed you or something." Bart smiled.

Duxter left the outfitter's and began his journey. He began in an uplifted mood, but it wasn't long before he realized the size of Nowhere. The longer he walked the more concerned he became. He walked for miles, stumbling down hills, looking for a sign, for something to follow. He saw nothing. He continued over dunes, the unbearable heat of the sand penetrating the soles of his shoes. With his head down to protect his face, he noticed a trail of several footprints. He followed the prints for many miles until the tracks split, a single track continuing, the others going off in another direction. Why would one person split from a group and the others go their separate ways?

Part 2
Past Focus – Present Action

"A state of being where a person's energy is directed to the way things USED TO BE, or where present situations are blamed on past experiences. The person is unable to move into the future without somehow always keeping in view the past."

The Duxter Companion

Duxter Encounters a Stuck State

On closer examination of the single track, Duxter concluded the person must be walking backward. Could this be? He followed that set of prints for many more miles.

Suddenly, out of the middle of nowhere, appeared a fence. Now of course, Nowhere was somewhere and in fact could be anywhere, but a fence that cut Nowhere in half… that was strange.

He saw in front of him, a Being resting against the fence.

"Ohhhh…Ohhhh!… ," said the voice. "I'm SO tired. Won't *somebody* help me? I am helpless."

Duxter moved cautiously forward.

"Ohhhh!" cried the voice again.

There, stuck at the base of the fence, was a Being in such an attitude as would indicate despair and grief, head on its knees and arms wrapped around its legs.

"Hello," said Duxter, with concern in his voice.

"Ohhhh…," cried the Being, looking up at Duxter.

"What is the matter?" asked Duxter.

"I am stuck on this spot. I can go no further. I was with a group of fellow travellers and I stopped for a rest. But they continued on without me. Pretty soon it got dark and I was all alone."

"Why did you not get up and follow them?" asked Duxter.

"I did but this is as far as I was able to go," explained the Being.

"I see." Though Duxter did not "see", he felt it was the only thing to say.

"I...I... can walk only backwards, facing only where I have been before. And so I backed into this obstacle, and here I sit, not able to go back, and yet prevented from going forward by this barrier."

"But it is just a fence, easily passed by following to the left or right. Better yet, why not just go back to where you were?" exclaimed Duxter excitedly, believing he could help the person by giving the solution.

The Being did not seem to be listening.

"It is impossible. Then I would be walking forward, back from where I came and since I can walk only backward, I can go only forward to where I am going. I therefore can go nowhere at all." That explanation seemed to be exhausting and the Backwards Being curled up into a tight, protective ball. It slumped, its head falling further into its chest.

Duxter stopped to ponder the explanation and then asked: "But why do you walk backward?" Obviously the only question to ask.

"This is a barren and frightening place. I turn my head to the left and the right and see only desert, weird shapes, objects I have never encountered before. But when I face backward, I see light, comfort, and a place I long for again. So I walk backward to keep that place in sight. It is comforting to me."

Duxter did not say anything. There was nothing to say. Nothing he could think of doing. He could not carry the person, for he did not know where the Backwards Being was going. He could not guide the Backwards Being out. Anyway, he was not really sure that the Backwards Being wanted to be guided anywhere. So he sat and pondered the predicament.

"What if I helped pull you up?"

He did not wait for an answer. Grabbing the Being around its waist, Duxter heaved. The Being began to lift, but it was glued to the spot like strands of gooey bubblegum stuck to the bottom of a shoe. He could lift the Being just so high, then its dead weight would snap it back to the ground with a thud.

The Being groaned. "It's no use." They stopped to think things through. Duxter's ears picked up the sound of a motorcyle buzzing over the sand dunes. He looked up to see a trail of dust following the motorcyle rider as he approached. Duxter was no longer surprised at what the desert of Nowhere presented to him. Several minutes later, a rider skidded to a stop in front of them. He wore goggles and a small leather flying helmet. His face was dusty. He was also wearing a long coat which he unbuttoned, exposing workers' coveralls. He got off his motorcycle and started walking towards them. Duxter looked at the box attached behind the seat.

THE CLEANER

We clean up your past
Our speciality - Unwanted Skeletons

The Cleaner handed his card to Duxter. "When you're ready to clean up your past," he said and continued walking over to the Backwards Being.

"Why does he think I need to do that?" Duxter asked himself.

"OK. What do we have here?" The Cleaner took out his glasses and knelt down next to the Backwards Being. "Hmmm. Your past finally caught up to you, did it?" He laughed. The Backwards Being frowned. "This happens all the time when people are under stress. They will very often revert back to long established coping strategies. The problem is, what worked once in the past can get in the way later on as life gets more complex and goals are more significant. So, how are you feeling?"

"Fine, I guess. I was walking backward to keep my past in view and…"

"No need to explain," replied the Cleaner. "I don't need to know the details. What happened doesn't matter. What matters is what you want to do about it now."

"I tried to lift him up," interrupted Duxter "but he wouldn't budge. There seems to be a stuckness holding him to the ground, a gooey, stringy substance."

"Ah, yes. I've seen that before. It lets you get only so far before it snaps you back. Difficult. Can you raise yourself for me?"

The Being struggled to raise himself. The Cleaner looked carefully at the stuckness. "Hmmm, man you really are stuck, aren't you?" He stood up and paced the ground, deep in thought. Then he went to his motorcycle and opened his tool kit. He began to unload tools—a shovel, a blowtorch, large wire cutters. Nothing seemed to be the right tool for the job. He opened a side pannier bag and rummaged through. "Ahh, here it is." He took out a small mirror.

"Take a look at yourself."

The Backwards Being looked carefully at himself and where he was.

"Ya. I see I'm stuck. I already knew that," he exclaimed rather righteously. "What are you going to do about it?" he asked.

"No," said the Cleaner. "Look closer at the absurdity of the situation." The Being looked closer and he snorted, then chuckled. "Look at what is really stopping you. A fence, nothing more."

The Backwards Being started to laugh. His laugh was rich and deep.

"So what would you like me to do?" asked the Cleaner.

The Backwards Being sat still and looked fondly off into the distance, a slight smile on his face. "It wasn't that the past was particularly good," he responded, "it's just more comfortable than where I am now."

The Cleaner nodded his head, though didn't say a word.

"I'm just not sure if…"

"That's OK. Take your time. It's just that life will be richer if you do choose to move, but people don't always want that. I don't clean up every past I see. Some people are not ready yet. They still have too much invested in holding onto it."

Silence filled the space between all of them. Duxter wondered why the Backwards Being was taking so long to make up his mind.

"OK. Get me loose. I'm ready. Let's do it," the Being said, growing more excited. The Cleaner patted his shoulder as he stood up to look through his tools.

"What tool? What tool?" he said, absentmindedly. "This job requires a delicate touch," he said to no one in particular while rummaging through his bag. "The stuckness will begin to solidify soon. So we need to be quick. Aha! Here it is."

Duxter couldn't tell what the Cleaner was carrying.

"This," he said, "is the only thing that will do the job." He reached into his box for rubber gloves and safety glasses, which he put on. "Just a precaution," he said. "Been using this stuff for years, even clean my oven with it."

"Wow! It must be pretty powerful," remarked Duxter.

"Yup, it's all natural. Smells pretty bad too. Though my mother swears by it." The Cleaner unscrewed the top of the bottle and put a small amount into the cap.

"What is it? Some sort of an acid or chemical?" asked the Backwards Being, nervously, regretting for a second his decision.

"No. Vinegar and water," the cleaner said nonchalantly.

"Vinegar! But I'm stuck!"

"You sound disappointed. Am I supposed to make a big production out of this?"

"No, but I just thought because of my past it would take more work."

"Sorry to disappoint you. People always think their past is a bigger deal than it really is. Here, get up as far as you can go." He poured the vinegar onto the stuckness. It immediately started to fizzle and steam. The Being began to pull.

"Don't push it, just let it happen," the Cleaner remarked. Before too long, the Being was standing straight.

"I'm free! I feel so light, like a weight has been lifted. I can't believe it. Thank you so much!" he said, vigorously shaking the Cleaner's hands and then Duxter's.

"So it's time for me to pack up," said the Cleaner, getting up to go.

"Just a minute, what do I owe you?"

"Oh, I'm paid through my employer. Keep your money."

"Before you go," interrupted Duxter, "can I ask why you suggested I should need you?"

"I didn't say you need me at all. Plenty of people never clean up their past, but the past always intervenes in some way in the present. Sometimes in an obvious way like we have seen here today, sometimes it is just a film of dust on the person, hardly perceptible." He paused.

"What do you mean?" queried Duxter.

Duxter Encounters a Stuck State

"The dust is barely perceptible because it is your accumulated history. It has a powerful affect over you, but you are barely aware of its influence. When you react negatively towards something or someone, this is the dust. Take relationships, for instance. Is there someone at work you don't get along with but need to?"

Duxter thought of Smith. "Well, sure."

"It may be that something happened a while back that influenced the relationship right off the bat, a preconceived idea, a belief, a stereotype, or a judgement created by an action or inaction. Maybe it happened so long ago that you don't even remember now, but the perception stuck with you just the same. The perception is the dust. Or it could be that the person reminds you of someone from your past. It could be the way she walks, the tone of her voice. Anything may trigger a response that is unconscious, but has repercussions in the present. You, Duxter, have this film around you right now."

Duxter looked worried and began dusting himself off.

"I noticed it right away. Everyone has it. But it's only worth doing something about if it limits you in some way."

Duxter relaxed immediately. "So you don't have to do anything about it?"

"I don't care what you do. Just when you're ready give me a call. Well, I'm off." He jumped on his motorcycle, pulled his goggles over his eyes, and roared off in a cloud of dust.

Duxter watched the Backwards Being enjoying his new found freedom. "There doesn't seem to be too much more for me to do." Duxter said to himself.

"So," said Duxter, "I guess I better be off too. Are you coming?"

"No. I'm going to sit here awhile. I'll be fine. Thank you so much for your help."

"It was nothing, really. Goodbye, then." Duxter felt uneasy at leaving but, knowing that the Being could now make choices for itself, he turned his mind to his own journey. The words "take from the past only what you need for the future" flashed through his mind. He thought he felt the knapsack vibrate.

As he walked along in the middle of Nowhere he once again became aware of the nothingness around him, nothing save for the fence. It went on for miles in all directions. He decided to follow the fence to the right. The longer he walked, the more he seemed to be going nowhere. This, of course, was not too surprising.

Opening a Gate to a New Adventure

S oon, in the distance, he saw a sign that resembled a sign such as one would see on a highway. It was quite large with big bold letters that said:

> **GATE AHEAD. OPEN AT OWN RISK**

Duxter had walked too far and was feeling so frustrated at getting nowhere that, although the sign spoke of possible danger, it was at least a change from the boredom. He continued walking until up ahead he saw an arrow pointing to a handle. The gate was unmanned but had a sign nailed to it.

> **YOU ARE NOW ENTERING
> THE STATE OF CAN'T**

If Duxter had a map with him, he would have realized that Nowhere was made up of a series of states, one of which was CAN'T.

He opened the gate and walked in. He felt at last that he was getting somewhere.

Unlike Nowhere, Can't was not barren but, to the far horizon, it was filled with signs—signs that dictated what couldn't be done.

"You can't walk on the grass."

"You can't do such and such… you're too old."

"Don't climb that tree, you can't reach the first branch."

One even said, "You can't enter the State of Can't."

Duxter looked around in shock. He had been told of this place all his life, at school, at work, by the family. But he had never believed such a place could actually exist. It was, in fact, a very limiting state. Very little, if anything, was allowed and what was allowed was restricted to what was believed to be not possible. As the truth of his situation sank in he wished that he had read the signs more carefully. He found himself reaching back for the handle of the gate.

"How did I get here? Why am I here?" he asked himself out loud.

"Why, that's easy to answer."

"What? Who is that?" cried Duxter, turning quickly around to look.

"I said, that is easy to answer."

"Who are you?" asked Duxter, quite surprised to be answered, and looking down on an officious gentleman in a top hat.

"Let me introduce myself," said the man in the hat. "My name is Ulysses Can't," or "U. Can't for short. I am the associate head and official emissary of CAN'T. It is my duty to introduce new arrivals to our state. My associate, Ignatius Can't, is away on business, recruiting new patriots, and sends his regrets that he couldn't be here to greet you as well. He was very much looking forward to this day, but I can't be in two places at once now, can he?" (U called his associate I for short.)

U. Can't stuck out his hand in greeting. "You may remember I. Can't from a Christmas party at your place of business. I was very impressed with your lack of belief in yourself and felt you would get along quite well here in the State of Can't."

"You sent me the ticket?" asked Duxter, incredulously.

"No, I did. He recruited you personally. He talked for weeks of your impending arrival."

Duxter felt betrayed and cheated.

"Young fellow," U. Can't said, putting his arm around Duxter, pushing him along, "the answer to your query is very simple. You chose to be here. Everyone who comes here chooses."

"Forgive me but I would not choose to come to a place that is obviously so restrictive. I can't do anything. In fact, I was told I can't even be here."

"Then why did you choose to go Nowhere?"

"I didn't choose, it just happened. One moment I was in my bedroom, the next I was on the desert floor."

"So you didn't answer the advertisement?"

"Yes, but…"

"And you didn't pick up the phone?"

"Well, sure, but…"

"And you didn't use the ticket?"

"Why, of course, but…"

"So, really, what you are saying is that you have no free will to choose? Oh, how wonderful!" U said, ringing his hands in delight. "I was right, you *are* a good candidate."

Now thoroughly confused, Duxter asked if there was a place where he could rest.

"All in good time, my friend, all in good time." They walked along for some time. Duxter looked around the city he was in. It looked no different from any other city. People bustled along, seemingly going about with purpose and direction.

U. Can't talked excitedly about his State, his pride at how clean the city was, no crime, no sadness, no pain. It was a city of contented people. "Surely," he concluded, "It was exactly what Duxter was looking for."

As they continued to walk, citizens bowed their heads respectfully and parted as U and Duxter walked on. It seemed unhealthy to Duxter that U should have so much power over anyone.

"What makes it so safe," U went on, "is that everyone knows his or her boundaries and feels comfortable knowing what can't be done. After all, life shouldn't be hard should it? I and myself are the caretakers. The rules are quite simple, really."

"You mean you and I dictate every action?" Duxter asked, incredulously.

"Isn't that the way it is? We all tell each other what can't be done rather than what can be done. You, for instance," pointing his finger at Duxter, "have told your own son many times that something was impossible. What about the time he wanted to go to rock climbing camp and you said it would be too dangerous. Are you not dictating what can't be done?"

"Yes but that was dif…"

"Of course you are, Duxter, my friend. Come, we are almost at the hotel. One last thing," his expression changed, "we will tell you what can't be done and you will believe it." He stared right into Duxter's eyes not smiling, no expression at all. It was a command. "Let me get the door." He was smiling once again.

The hotel Manager bowed to U. Can't and greeted Duxter like a regular patron.

He shook his hand warmly.

"We have been expecting you. We have reserved a suite on the top floor for your enjoyment. You will find the view of the city extraordinary from that height." He snapped his fingers and the Bellhop appeared. "Please relieve Mr Hexter of this extra baggage he has been carrying around. He will not need it here. Show him to his suite." The Bellhop bowed. All Duxter was carrying was the knapsack, so a reference to baggage confused him. But the funny thing was he did seem lighter. He looked over at the Bellhop. He seemed to move slower, as if he was carrying the weight of the world on his shoulders.

"I sincerely hope you enjoy your stay," the Manager called.

Duxter was starting to feel bewildered. What was going on here? How did they know his name? Why was he staying at this hotel? And where was he really?

Before any questions could be asked, he was ushered up the elevator to follow U. Can't and the Bellhop like a lost puppy, looking for a new home.

His room was large and quite comfortable. The Bellhop opened the curtains to an expansive view of the city. It struck Duxter that no building except this hotel was over five stories in height. Looking around the room, Duxter noticed the suite contained four rooms including a kitchen, living room, dining room and bedroom. The furniture was quite comfortable. Nothing was out of place and everything was nailed down to the floor. Duxter smiled, thinking back to the outpost and how everything had been stuck to the shelves.

"You will, no doubt, discover things that you will need," said the Bellhop. "Please just ring and I will be here for you." The Bellhop did not stay for a tip. Rather, he quietly closed the door of the room and was gone.

"Please," said U. "Make yourself at home. You will want for nothing. You will have to do nothing. You will never have to feel badly again. Happiness is our desire for you. We want your stay here to be as pleasant as possible. U clapped his hands together. "So, I must leave now, but if there is anything I can do, please let me know. You will find clothes in the closet and toiletries in the bathroom. Oh yes, your stay in the hotel will be short until we find a more permanent residence for you. "Good-bye my friend," U said, wringing his hands and muttering his pleasure at Duxter's arrival.

The door clicked shut. Duxter was alone.

He was too flabbergasted to talk. The questions he had and the confused feelings! What was he to do? His fatigue was overwhelming.

He did what he usually did. He went to bed to sleep.

Some time later (who knows how long, who really cares), Duxter awoke. Feeling refreshed, if still confused, he decided to find out more about this place. He wasn't sure what he was going to do, but he did know he didn't want to stay here too much longer.

He went for a walk.

The street was like any other to be found in a large city. A bustling crowd of ordinary looking people, people he would see at work or in his own home town.

What stood out were the signs.

The farther he walked, the more restrictive the signs were. It became clear that he could do nothing but follow the crowd as it moved along. He passed corner after corner, building after building, the crowds pushed him along. He was being moved against his will, caught up in the movement and unable to do anything but follow it. He felt he was losing control, which of course he was. The State of Can't was taking over.

Up ahead he noticed a very large building, taking up two city blocks. People moved in and out of it carrying luggage and cases. He fought the Can't and its seductive power. As a gap opened up in the crowd he stumbled into a train station. It was a cavernous building with waves of people following a sign down a marble staircase. The voice echoed from a loudspeaker way up in the rafters.

"Last call for passengers leaving CAN'T for WON'T!" boomed the loudspeaker.

"ALL ABOARD!"

The people in the crowd started to run. Others looked frantically at their watches while standing in line at ticket counters.

The schedule noted that this train should make it to WON'T in three hours, but only if it wanted to.

Along the walls travel posters called out to passers by, enticing them to exotic locales—

"Visit the Leaning Tower of Skepticism!"

"The Healing Waters of SHOULDN'T can't be missed!"

Duxter spotted a map on the wall. He gravitated towards it, hoping it might give him a way out of there.

The map outlined all the States of Nowhere, Can't being at the centre, with Assumption, Disbelief, Doubt, Fear, Shouldn't, Won't, I'm Not _____ Enough to _____ (you fill in the blanks), surrounding it. What was strange to

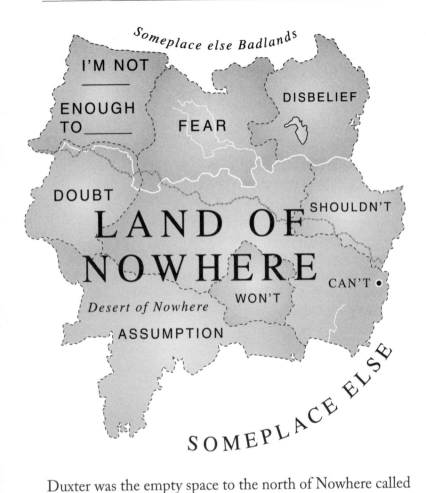

Duxter was the empty space to the north of Nowhere called the "Bad Lands". If there was anything out there, no one from Can't had ever mapped it out or wanted to know about it, for all the roads and train tracks ended suddenly at the border. Maybe this was the place he needed to get to, though "how" was the question. It seemed as if this territory was off limits to the citizens. Hmmm… He wasn't going to get anywhere going by train, he concluded.

Back out on the street, he noticed things had changed. He was unable to find any landmarks. Had he gone out another exit? Maybe being swept along with the crowds had prevented him from really seeing where he was going. Moreover, he did not know how to get back to his hotel.

He looked around to get his bearings and noticed official looking guides with the letters "T.S." on their shirtsleeves, directing people. He thought they might be able to help him find his way back to the hotel.

"Excuse me. I am not too sure where I am going. Could you direct me to the…"

"I recommend you go that way." Out went the arm pointing north.

"But I haven't told you where I want to go…"

"Go that way… ," said the official, pointing again to the north.

"But…"

"That way." The conversation was over. Someone else asked for directions. Duxter went north as the official had said.

He walked on and asked three more guides. Each gave him a different recommendation as to the best direction he should go. Each direction was different, each was wrong.

Duxter was tired and frustrated at going around in circles, being told by everyone which direction he should travel but not getting anywhere. He was so tired he decided to sit down on the next available bench and get control of his thoughts.

Duxter Makes a Choice

He had been sitting for quite some time when up ahead he saw a person walking towards him. This was not a corner guide. The person seemed to want to talk to him. The person sat down next to Duxter and smiled. "Good afternoon," he said.

Duxter was in no mood to be cordial. "Who might you be?"

"I am William Powers. My friends call me Will. I am a member of a small band of individuals who believe that one can, if one wants to. We call ourselves the rebels of CAN."

"What do you mean?" exclaimed Duxter. "Of course you can. That seems so obvious."

"Does it?" retorted Will. "Then why are you here in the land of Can't?"

"Augghh, not you too! Okay, okay I… I… walked through a gate and here I am," replied Duxter indignantly.

"Yes, yes," said will, ignoring Duxter's emotional outburst. "But the only way to pass through the gate is through Nowhere and why did you choose to travel there?"

"I don't know anymore," Duxter sighed dropping his head into his chest. "U Can't said I chose to be here but I did not choose. It just happened. One minute I was at home and the next I was sitting on top of a sand dune. It happened right after I had finished reading a letter I had received from my travel agency explaining that I had chosen to go Nowhere. It was at that moment that I realized I was responsible for my own travel arrangements and indeed was wasting my travel time and had been for quite some time."

"Hmmm... Yes, you see, you did choose. And that is my point. You chose to go to Nowhere and arrived as soon as you realized it."

"HUH," responded Duxter, the dawn of understanding seeping into his consciousness. "I know this is going to sound obvious to you, but I had to realize I was here before I could be here?"

"Right! Let's say you had decided to visit a new city. You may only know you were in that city if you recognized a sign telling you what city it was or by noticing a familiar landmark. Otherwise you may not realize you were there. In fact you had been nowhere for quite some time, aimlessly going to work, feeling miserable, jealous when your colleague got promotions, and wanting to escape, when I Can't forced you to answer his questions at the Christmas party."

"How do you know so much about me?" interrupted Duxter. "Everyone knows more about me than I do!"

"Oh, we have been keeping our eye on you for some time. We knew that U and I had targeted you for arrival and we wanted to help you. But we also know that you have the potential to break out of here and help us to bring about a state of growth."

"You mean you have been following me around, and you let me stumble into this awful place?" exclaimed Duxter, furious that he had been made to look a fool.

"We have always been with you from the very beginning, watching but not interfering. You see we had to wait for the right time. We could not afford to have the Can't brothers discover our group. But more importantly, we had to make sure you were ready to listen to us and help us. Not everybody we have contacted has been co-operative. Not everyone has been ready. Some people are not willing to look objectively at the State of Can't and see it for what it is. A very powerful ugly brutal state, where free will is subjugated through the T.S. police and the treacherously simple rules and regulations. U and I look after your every whim and protect you from harm by dictating what you cannot do. It is that simple. You see," said Will continuing, "you go wherever you decide to go. Your goal was to come here. Had you chosen a different destination, you would have gone SOME-PLACE ELSE just as effortlessly."

"Someplace else?" Duxter suddenly remembered the map on the wall of the train station. "That's where I want to go! Well, how do I get there? I have been trying but I always get pointed in another direction. I almost believe I can't get out."

"Of course you believe that, look where you are. They want you to believe it. Look, as soon as you believe it is true it is. It is a reciprocal relationship. They say it is not possible, you believe it and prevent yourself from doing it. It is devilishly clever."

"You mean U and I Can't?" asked Duxter

"Yes, them and the "They Say" police. I presume you have seen them on the street corner directing people where to go and therefore what to believe?"

" You mean those people with the T.S. emblem on their shirt sleeves?"

"Yes, those people. They are the most dangerous people in the state. They control what you think. It appears they are helping when they point the way but their directions are based on what they know and do not take your needs and considerations into account. They rarely have all the necessary information, and usually don't care if they don't. You may go to them for advice and they will gladly give it for that is their role as guide and officer, but if they really wanted to help they would ask you what *you* want, how *you* propose to get it and not tell *you* what *you* SHOULD do."

Duxter thought about this. Yes that explained why he was going in circles earlier on that day. It became evident to Duxter that there had always been people like that in his life. People who meant well but were not really helping at all. He recognized them because they themselves would say that they had heard from someone else that such and such was true, a fact, when in reality they were only projecting their own fears onto him.

They sat silently together for some time.

"We want you to join us. We want you to assist us in bringing about the downfall of this rule."

This hit Duxter like a ton of bricks. "A coup?" exclaimed Duxter. "You want me to help you overthrow the State of Can't? I can't do that!"

"Hmmm, so you say. But what if you *could*? What would you do to help us if you *could*? We think you can play a valuable role. We need your assistance, and you are obviously looking for a way out."

Yes, that was true. He did want to get out of there. He now knew that this was not a good place to be. To call it a police state was being too kind. But what could he do?

"What you can do will present itself to both of us. You will know soon enough. In every situation there are possibilities that become apparent as soon as the situation is looked at not as a problem but as a potential for action. I am not concerned. Trust yourself."

"Our numbers are very small but we are growing. We meet several miles from here in the forest. We live as outlaws, but the valley is off limits to the inhabitants of the State of Can't for it is unknown to them."

Unbeknownst to Duxter or Will, a member of the T.S. Police had been watching them. They had been warned to be on the look out for a tall wiry fellow whose actions were not consistent with the average inhabitant. They had been informed of a small pesky band of people who could create problems for the city state. Could this be the fellow? The policeman started to walk over. Will finally noticed the T.S. Police out of the corner of his eye. He looked around and decided that it was time to go.

"Duxter, don't look around; act normal. We are going to stand up and start walking toward those bushes over yonder. It appears we have been followed and we must make our escape. Up ahead is an opening in the bushes. Head toward that and enter it. I will go in another direction and meet up with you on the other side to take you into the safety of the valley. Go now!"

Duxter's heart started to pound as he walked toward the bushes. He felt as though he was being split in two. Half of him wanted to turn and run. The other half knew he should stay as calm as possible and walk straight into the bushes.

"I can't do this. I shouldn't do this. Things are not that bad. They are taking care of me. I am not that badly off! Stay and enjoy the comforts of this state. No decisions to be made, no worries." He heard U CAN'T voices in his head."

Duxter continued to walk on. His mind went back to the letter he had received from I. Can't. "Congratulations for choosing…" Choice! Oh God, I don't want choice, too many things to consider, too many possibilities for failure. I just want it the way it used to be. Before I received the letter. Now I am on the run from something I don't understand, going somewhere I don't know about, to someone I don't know. Duxter stopped in his tracks. For a moment he was unable to move. He was stuck, indecisive and confused…

Duxter broke through the hedge and found Will waiting for him on the other side.

"Duxter I am so pleased you chose to join us," exclaimed Will, patting Duxter on the back. "Come, let me show you where you are going."

Duxter was in a state of confusion and was agitated. Why did he have to go through the bushes alone?

It was a little time before Duxter and Will came to a spot overlooking a long expansive jungle.

"We meet down here because the state can't find us," laughed Will. The humor of the statement was lost on Duxter. He was still thinking about his choice. He stopped to face Will.

"I had to go through the bush by myself. You were supposed to help me."

"I did," replied Will. "I told you how to break free. It was your choice to heed my suggestion or to stay. By the way it was a fabulous decision you made. You should be very proud. Instead, you seem angry with me, as if I was supposed to hold your hand and protect you. You don't seem to understand that YOU are in control. Your power lies in your 'wilfulness.' When you begin to understand this, you will be free as never before." Duxter was shocked at this response. It was as if Will had thrown water on his face and stopped him in his tracks.

They stumbled on down a very narrow path that seemed to disappear into the trees. He could not really see the trail markings so he asked Will.

"Oh there are none, in fact we are not really following a trail at all. How could we be? We are creating one as we go along."

"Just a second, then how do you know we are going in the right direction?" asked Duxter, ready to go back.

"Duxter, let go of your fear. Be open to the possibilities the path is presenting to us. I will tell you that the camp is in that direction. We are heading that way. Whatever happens between here and there, have the confidence to know that you will handle it. We will handle it together."

"But how do you know? We may be getting lost or taking a wrong turn. I wouldn't know. What if we never get there? What if...?"

"To make it out of the State of Can't will require you to begin trusting your own decisions and to be open to the reality of the present situation and the possibilities that it offers. That state of mind is a practised skill that becomes a habit. We are beginning your learning right now as we go along."

Duxter looked skeptical. All this talk of letting go and being in the moment made no sense to him whatsoever. It all seemed like hog wash.

"Duxter, trust in yourself and your decision. Let go of your worries. You decided to press forward rather than stay behind. You are already going in a new direction, so how do you know you are NOT going the right way?" responded Will.

In frustration Duxter responded, "You tell me to let go and begin trusting myself. But it is you I need to trust to show me the way to the camp."

Will laughed, "Boy you sure are stubborn and argumentative, every time you doubt yourself you slow your progress. Your frustration actually prevents you from acting in your best interest. So rather than wasting your energy you may want to stop and practise what I suggested."

There was a long silence. "I don't know how." Duxter dropped his head in shame.

"AHH! Excellent, Well done!" cried Will. "That is the

first step. Look Duxter, please understand you are experiencing what everyone, including me, did when faced with the prospect of the freedom of Free Will. When I experienced release from Can't, I was confused and very uncomfortable. I fought to stay small and safe again. Then I said what you just said. I don't know how! Those few words meant I was prepared to walk into discovering new things and ideas, and let go of my fears."

"Oh boy," Duxter let out his breath "What have I got myself into? Everything is becoming topsy-turvy. You congratulate me for not knowing, yet to me that is a problem. You tell me to let go and at the same time you tell me I am in control. This makes absolutely no sense."

"Excellent, stay with the confusion, it's perfectly natural. It's a new part of you coming to the surface, the part that is trying to understand the paradox."

"What paradox?"

"The paradox that says, the more you try and control things through frustration and anger, the less control you actually have. Conversely, the more you let go of your fears and control the more control you ultimately have. Wild, huh? Don't even bother trying to understand it intellectually. Rather experience it instead."

"How do I do that?"

"Wonderful question! Boy are you moving ahead quickly! Here's what you do. Stop, take a deep breath, let it out slowly and listen to the jungle."

Duxter did as he was told. At first, he heard silence and then, as he began to focus his attention away from himself, he began to hear birds and animals, leaves blowing in the wind and finally he picked up human voices, a little way off. "Hey, I hear people up ahead, they are coming from that direction. Let's go find them," he exclaimed.

Will laughed and followed Duxter until they broke through the clearing and they saw a group of a dozen or so men and women sitting around the fire talking and laughing.

" ...and that is the way it must be if we are going to succeed." Duxter looked around at the speaker. Was it a he or a she? In the firelight he was unable to tell. Duxter was unable to pick up the thread of the discussion but whatever had been said was creating a stir. Little groups were forming to debate the finer points. It was evident to Duxter that the meeting was winding down as many stoodup and stretched.

Will whispered, "Don't worry Duxter. You didn't miss too much. At least nothing we can't tell you later after you get your bearings and catch your breath."

Duxter looked around the encampment. It became obvious to him that there were no houses, in fact no buildings of any kind.

"Where do people live?" asked Duxter.

"We go back to the city. We have to, if we are going to have any opportunity to overthrough it. Every week we gather at this spot to plan our strategy and implement our attack. But every other day we move and act just like all the others at the State of Can't, except that we work hard at infiltrating Can't and destroying its power."

Duxter Meets the Bellhop

"Come over here. I would like you to meet someone," said Will taking Duxter by the arm. "Meet your partner for the next while." Duxter recognized the person as the Bellhop at the hotel. He was still dressed in his uniform. A navy pillbox cap with chinstrap. Red waistcoat with two rows of brass buttons. Navy slacks with a red stripe running down the side.

"Hi, Duxter. It's good to see you again." Duxter's jaw dropped. "You look surprised to see me." Chuckling Will left them to talk to someone else.

"Well you are just a…" responded Duxter, slightly mistrusting.

"So you believe that I am not capable of affecting growth?"

"No, but… I was expecting… I don't know…"

The Bellhop smiled, "In fact, that is our strategy for overthrowing Can't. We all have unassuming roles in the city. Some of us are administrators, others are community workers, still others own businesses. The people you see here tonight make up a small percentage of all those who have chosen to fight the battle. What is tricky for us is to maintain our goal of overthrowing the State of Can't while remaining integrated in the community."

"How do you do it?"

"Part of our success comes from our passion and belief in what we are doing. But another comes from the clarity of our vision. All of us know what the end result looks like. Each one of us can see it, hear it and feel it. We do not focus on change itself, rather on possibility. In this case the possibility of a free state." His voice was starting to rise. "Just imagine the city with no T.S. Police. No one dictating what cannot be done. The signs are gone, the land is free and the people have choice."

Just then Will came over to save Duxter. "Is he giving you the 'Just Imagine' speech?" He laughed and patted the Bellhop on the arm. The Bellhop frowned. "Duxter, this kind of passion is critical to our success and I wish it was found in everyone. He has probably influenced more people than just about any one of us and has certainly recruited most of the people here tonight." Duxter looked at the Bellhop with growing respect.

The Bellhop continued. "Let me say that it is by improving the small things, working on the simple things, that we bring about the possibility we all want. We build a momentum of successes until we can tackle the big things. No one is going to overthrow the State of Can't in a quick swipe and expect it to remain permanently changed. Although I am only a Bellhop, I come in contact with hundreds of people every day whom I can affect in some positive way."

"Forgive me," Duxter said. "I obviously have a lot to learn. What is this word 'possibility'?"

"Most people talk of needing to change something. The Bellhop went on. "We talk of the possibility of something new and different."

"What is the difference?" asked Duxter feeling they were splitting hairs of language.

"For us, possibility implies growth, development something exciting and new. The very essence of which propels us forward. Change demotivates. Always talking about change is tiresome and boring. Let's talk instead about growth and the possibility of possibility."

Duxter thought about the idea of possibility. What was

his possibility? Moving up in the company? Starting a small business? Writing children's books? What did he want to do?

"How do I know what my possibility looks like?" asked Duxter.

"You will recognize it when you see it. Everyone's possibility is different. For me it's a large and friendly beast that doesn't stand too tall, but is extremely powerful, present and accounted for everyday. Through it I can achieve a world of Can. Possibilities can be very elusive, and difficult to see if you are not open to seeing them. It sometimes shows itself to you when you are least expecting it. So the best thing you can do right now is be open to its existence."

Will who was still listening nodded his agreement. "If you will excuse me, I have some last minute details to take care of before our meeting is over." He walked over to the fire.

"If I may have your attention?" All talking stopped. Will, thought Duxter, is obviously an important person. "Let us, as usual, leave in pairs over the next hour. Go back through the exit north of here. Some of you will meet back here again next week. Others will not meet here again for a while. You will all be contacted in the usual way. Take care and God speed." Everyone nodded as if they knew and had been prepared ahead of time, everyone except Duxter.

"But where is the north exit and when will my time be?" asked Duxter.

"Your time will be in five days. I will come and get you," replied the Bellhop.

As they were walking back to the city, it struck Duxter that the Bellhop was the perfect person to help him.

"I would like to apologize for my surprise earlier this evening. It was rude of me to think that you could not be of service to me. I did not realise how useful being a Bellhop could be to the process of change."

"Not change, growth Duxter!" interrupted the Bellhop. "There's a fundamental difference which you will discover soon enough. Anyway, we are all around, being of service. All one need do is ask. We are not always as obviously dressed as I am." He was pointing to his pill box hat and uniform. "You will find those you need to meet when you are ready. What is important is that you be open to the possibility."

Duxter nodded. He said that he always felt that he had to do things himself. When he was under stress or in the process of change, his natural response was to go inward.

The Bellhop said he understood. He called it "being in your head." He continued, "When under stress, all of our energy can be transferred to our thoughts. It is almost overwhelming at times. Some of us lose the physical connection with the body and perhaps sit in front of the television alone with our thoughts. While others of us need to do things; clean, fix something, work with our hands, go for a drive, be physically active. In either case, being 'in our head' is not productive. Especially if the thoughts just sit there inside, taking up valuable space."

"But, if you are thinking about your problem, is that not good?"

"This is not about good or bad, Duxter. It is about handling the issue effectively, using strategies that will be useful. Holding onto your negative thoughts is very rarely useful. Rather, it is better to put them somewhere. Let them float in the air and get blown away with the wind. Store them on paper, whatever. Come, let me show you." He took Duxter over to a large hole, some distance from the fire pit. It was boarded up. "This hole is where we go when we are 'in our heads.' It is filled with all those thoughts that prevent us from doing our tasks. All we do is yell or talk into the hole as loudly or softly as we choose. It sometimes gets filled with tears that flood it out. But the great thing about this hole is that the thoughts disappear forever into the ground like rain water after a storm. This hole gives us permission to whine and complain and then get on with our goals again. Imagine giving yourself permission to complain and then picking yourself up again, full of life and vigour. This is what the pit is for. Would you like to see?"

Duxter did not really want to see it, but knew that the idea of releasing unproductive thoughts was useful. It cleared the mind, relaxed the thoughts and provided an outlet to clear thinking again.

The Bellhop lifted the top. Duxter looked down. Way at the bottom he noticed something move.

"What is that down at the bottom?"

"Those are 'word munchers'. They eat all of the words and sounds that fill the pit. In effect they are scavengers that keep the pit clean, for the next person. Could you imagine the sounds that would seep out of the hole if those creatures didn't do their job? It would be so loud we wouldn't hear ourselves think." The Bellhop recovered the hole. It was time to go.

By the time Duxter returned to his room, it was late or was it early? Five days later he received a note from the Bellhop.

Your time is now. Go to the park bench and walk straight into the woods following the path that will present itself to you. Trust yourself, Duxter. I will be there.

The Bellhop

Duxter Encounters the
Tree Top Nuisances

As he walked into the jungle, he began to hear a cacophony of sounds all around his head. High up in the trees monkeys were chattering away in a lively discussion.

He stopped to listen.

"Maybe I shouldn't go," they seemed to be saying. "What if…" "But there is no path." "Trust yourself, you can do it." "It's time," went the conflicting sounds. Sounds that seemed to meld with his own doubt and struggle.

He looked up into the trees. The monkeys seemed to be mimicking him, his face, his actions. They were reflecting him. He pushed on faster, but the monkeys always kept up with him, swinging from tree to tree, chattering, chattering, chattering. Eventually, the path broke into the clearing of the group.

"But what tools are we going to use? What weapons have we?"

A woman looked up as Duxter arrived.

"Ah. Welcome Duxter. It is good to have you back. We are glad you chose to join us once again." It was the Elder. This time Duxter could see clearly it was a woman. Her face was so old yet so vibrant, the eyes naive and wise, ancient yet young.

"Please sit down."

"I would rather stand," Duxter responded, noticing others were standing.

"As you wish."

The meeting went on for some time. Talk was loud, heated and animated. It was clear that the group was of two minds. Some wanted to take a direct action approach, shock the system and take over with violence. Others felt that a continuation of the slow infiltration, person by person, goal by goal, success by success, was the most effective way.

The debate raged for what seemed hours. Duxter grew weary and moved off from the circle.

At breaking state, it struck Duxter that the debate was fruitless. The rebels, no matter what they did, would never overthrow the State of Can't. For if it did not exist, neither would Can. Each needed the other to define its existence. Yet the rebels' cause was far from useless, because on an individual level, growth could be made and through each individual the whole could be transformed. All of us, he thought, must ultimately fight our own wars, never alone, but ultimately responsible for all of our own actions. How we react to challenges placed in front of us is the issue.

His mind went back as if he was watching a movie of his past decisions and actions. He noticed those times when he was in charge and he noticed that his ability to bounce back from an event was important.

Questions, Questions, Questions.

The Bellhop joined him. "You look lost in thought, my friend." Duxter told him of his thoughts, his confusions, decisions he had made throughout his life, his joys and regrets, about his family and his wife, his career past and present. He laughed and cried and fell silent. It all came out in a torrent he was unable to control. He had never done this before. It was embarrassing but liberating just the same.

"Come, let me show you something." They started down a path away from the rebel stronghold.

"Go back over your life to a time when you felt a high level of energy and excitement, doing something you felt you could do forever and not stop. What were you doing?"

Duxter told him of his work with wood. The feel of it, the smell of it, using the tools, planning out the job, the satisfaction of seeing his completed job.

"This completion is important to you?"

"Well isn't it to everyone?" Duxter asked.

The Bellhop smiled. "Duxter, this is about you. You can like things that others do not, you know. We are searching for your unique need for satisfaction and fulfilment. So if completion is very important to you, so be it."

"Probably the most," interrupted Duxter.

"What else about working with wood excites you?"

"I like the environment, the smells, the texture of the wood. I get to stand up, move around, lift things."

"Tell me something. What is the environment at work like?"

"Well, I sit down all day in front of a computer terminal and on the phone. I rarely get to move around. I am not really using my creativity or hands in any way."

"So basically, you are telling me that your current position has very few qualities that you need in a job to be fulfilled and satisfied. Is that right?" Duxter nodded. "Is it any wonder then you feel unfulfilled in your current job? It must be an ongoing unfinished project."

Duxter nodded again.

"How do you ever know when you have done a truly great job?"

"Are you suggesting that I quit my job to become a carpenter? Because if you are, …".

"Easy Duxter, I am suggesting no such thing. I am merely pointing out that for you to be satisfied and probably more successful, any way you express yourself should include some of the qualities you told me about. Whether you are working with wood or not is hardly the issue. It is the qualities that are important."

The Bellhop gave Duxter a little anchor.

"This anchor represents all the important aspects that you must possess for you to feel fulfilled and satisfied. **Look back over your life and career, think about the anchors it offers you.** For every person out there, there are unique anchors."

Duxter took the anchor and stuffed it in his pocket. He didn't really seem to understand the conversation or the idea of a career anchor and its importance to job satisfaction. So the Bellhop tried a different approach.

"Duxter, what do you want? (When you are ninety years old and looking back over your life, what do

you see? What have you created?) These are questions to help you identify what is important to you."

"Not everyone," Duxter said, "is supposed to impact on the world. Not everyone will be powerful, successful in that 'star' kind of way. Some of us just want to do our jobs, enjoy our kids and be respected by our friends and family. That would make us happy."

"We are not talking about everyone. Don't hide behind the 'everyone' answer."

"How I live my life is very much dictated by my circumstances. I have little control over that."

"Is that so? Well then, I guess it is time for us to go back. We have made a mistake. I am sorry." He turned to go back.

"No, wait!" Duxter grabbed the Bellhop's arm. "I only mean that I have a lot of responsibilities. I sometimes feel trapped, much like the Being I saw back at the fence, unable to move forward."

"Why is it that you see those things you have included in your life as a limiting factor? Did they just show up one day and attach themselves to you? Surely they mean more to you than that?"

"Well no, I mean, yes. They do mean quite a bit but... I mean... what if I put them in peril? What if I am not capable of doing what I want?"

"What do you want?" the Bellhop challenged.

"To be happy..." Duxter let the thought trail off.

"And what will that get you?"

"Satisfaction, peace, recognition."

"So, you want satisfaction, peace and recognition?"

"Well sure, who doesn't?"

"Well, I don't. I want strength to handle adversity. I

want simplicity and serenity but not recognition. Again Duxter, these are your wants. This is about you, not anyone else. "So if you could have satisfaction, peace and recognition what would you need to do to achieve those qualities?"

"You mean in terms of work?"

"Could be or it could just be the way you live your life. You have created your life this far, you will be creating your life until you die. So you can choose to have satisfaction, peace and recognition or not. It is up to you."

"I feel that I have much more to offer the world. I have untapped potential that is just waiting to be released and used. Sometimes I feel like a racehorse banging at the gate just before the race. I see things I would like to play a part in. I would like to be on stage in front of an audience, maybe not professionally, maybe just for amateur theatre, I don't know."

"Yes, Duxter, you do know. You know exactly what you want, you always have. It has always been within you."

"Alright, if I think about it I do know, I guess I have always known, it's just that if I tell others they may laugh or not believe that I can do it."

"Yes," said the Bellhop, "it is always hard to describe to others what we want when we are not totally convinced of it ourselves."

"What do you mean?"

"What I mean is that people pick up on our confidence and commitment toward something. If they see incongruency, then their own confidence in the project will be less than committed. So let me ask you, what if those you love did not back you? What would you do?"

"I am not sure. I have thought of this often. I usually stop thinking about the future when this question comes up."

"Well, of course, if you have free will to create your life, then you have free will to talk about the issue or not."

Duxter nodded absentmindedly, hearing but not really listening to what the Bellhop was saying because they had gone as far as they could go. In front of them was a chasm. Not a wide chasm, but wide enough that to cross it would require a running jump and even then Duxter believed he would probably have to scramble up the chasm wall on the other side.

The Bellhop changed the subject.

"What would you need to do to cross this chasm?" the Bellhop asked, snapping Duxter back to reality.

"Why would I want to do that?"

All of a sudden Duxter heard the chattering monkeys overhead. "It's too far, it's very deep, so many challenges…" (he thought he heard them say.) "You can't accomplish that, you're nearly fifty."

"Because," said the Bellhop, "this is your way out. This is the only way out for you."

Duxter noticed a sign close to the edge.

CAUTION
A Leap of Faith is Required

"Ohhh no it's not. I will not jump this chasm. There must be another way. There has to be. You yourself said we have choice. There must be another way." Duxter went to the edge. He cautiously peered over it.

He looked down and saw a raging river far below. He wondered if there was a bridge, maybe a kilometre or two down river that he could cross, but none existed. He looked for a thinning of the gap, but there was none. The wall was uniform for many kilometres in either direction. The Bellhop turned to face Duxter and took him by the shoulders, staring him right in the eyes.

"Listen to me, Duxter. Sometimes after all the thinking and planning and worrying, talking and stalling, there is only one decision and that is to take action, Duxter! This is your action! You do have choice and you are more than welcome to stay here, but you won't be able to accomplish your purpose here with us. Your purpose lies back home with your family. You said yourself that we can never overthrow the State of Can't. But don't you see, you can! You are already doing so! It is time Duxter, it requires only your decision."

Duxter looked back at the sign

A Leap of Faith is Required

Funny... he thought he had read the word "caution" the first time. Hmm, maybe not.

"Let us, for a second, fantasize the possibility that you could jump this chasm and land safely on the other side," said the Bellhop. "What would you need to do? How would you prepare?"

But Duxter was getting tired. "It's time to go," he said. "I've seen enough."

They started heading back to the city. "Duxter", the bellhop continued, "there are five reasons why we don't always follow our Dreams. The Bellhop's thoughts can be distilled as follows:

- We are not yet ready to hear the message of our NIGGLE;
- We do not believe that what we WANT is really what we WANT;
- We are not supposed to want to do that according to our family influences, peer pressure, or preconceived ideas;
- We don't believe we have the skill, talent or resources to achieve it;
- It's not yet TIME.

Duxter was quiet all the way home but the chattering monkeys were louder than ever. Would they never stop?? He was not yet ready to hear the message.

Part 3
Future Focus – Present Action

"The State of being where the person's energy is focused on the way things WILL BE. He or she will make decisions and do things that move toward the future goal. This includes stopping to smell the proverbial roses at regular intervals."

The Duxter Companion

Duxter Finds a Note

Duxter was not sure how he got back to his room but there he was. On the bed lay a note, a clock and a strange book. He opened the note. It read:

Dear Duxter,

It should be no surprise to you that it is time. If you look closely at the clock you will see that this is so. Can you not see the obvious? Whatever you have been stalling on, whatever you have been afraid of, that is what you must take action upon. Duxter, as you sit reading this letter, imagine yourself accomplishing what you desire. See yourself making the leap, feel what you feel as you look back over your accomplishment. Feel the power, the energy, and the pride of it. Let it settle over you like a warm blanket. Surround yourself in its luxury. Imagine it now, Duxter. Use whatever that image may be to create the feeling of success.

Your Friends.

He saw himself make the leap. He felt his arms pumping and his legs carrying him closer to the edge. Over he went. Taking flight, he heard the air rushing by his ears, saw the land on the other side getting closer. He felt himself tumble as he landed. He saw that he could do it, it was possible. He had the will. He could see it now. It was within him.

He soon fell asleep with the image of his flight fixed in his mind.

"Let us for a second fantasize the possibility that you could jump this chasm and land safely on the other side, what would you need to do? How would you prepare? ..."

This question filled his dreams. He saw that he couldn't leap the chasm tomorrow because he wasn't fit enough. He knew that he would need to work at building up his strength. He had at least made the decision to jump anyway.

You see, what Duxter had forgotten long ago was the realization that achieving what we want doesn't happen overnight. All the worries he had shared with the Bellhop and I. Can't were merely barriers that, when broken down, contained the solutions and the path to his goal. And having realized that—he wanted it now! But he wasn't going to accomplish it now!

Time and patience are required, actions, small accomplishments that are recognized and celebrated, failures that are rewritten. Have patience, have purpose and recognize each accomplishment as a learning process that is critical to eventual success.

Out of the fogginess of his dream, the Bellhop appeared. He laughed and slapped Duxter on the back.

"Congratulations Duxter, you begin to see that your life's vision, by definition, will not always be your current reality. You will need to transform some things, to become, in a way, a new person. The 'you' that will leap over the chasm is stronger, more wilful. You are not yet that new you, not now, but you will be then."

The noise of the clock pierced his dream—WAKE UP, WAKE UP, WAKE UP!—it rang. He woke with a start. Looking at the clock closely, he could see that it was indeed time to wake up. The aroma of coffee filled his nostrils, yet there was no coffee pot in the room. He stretched and walked over to the window. The sky was overcast. "I hope it clears," he thought to himself. As he stretched, he noticed the book. It was about the size of a field guide, small enough to fit inside a jacket pocket. Its cover was of beautiful leather, the smell reminding him of a new pair of shoes. The pages were gilt edged and a red silk ribbon marker lay between them. Carefully he lifted the front cover.

The opening pages read as follows…

THIS IS YOUR COMPANION

How to take a Flying Leap and feel Good about it. Travels and Learnings for Now and Then.

This is the first volume of a two-volume set. It has been specifically designed for those of you who desire more from life. In it, you will find exercises and thoughts to complete. As in everything, a certain amount of focus will be required. We would suggest that you do it over a period of time. However, for those who wish the faster version, you can go directly to the most relevant sections.

Section 1 : For those who are unsure of what direction to leap, but know that a leap is required.

Section 2 : For those who know the direction of the leap but are unsure of the steps needed to make the leap.

Section 3 : For those who know what direction and how but are just unable to take the first step.

Duxter flipped through the book but each page was blank! There was nothing in it, no wisdom, no thoughts, no exercises, nothing. He threw the book onto the bed. Had he continued reading he would have been aware of the next paragraph...

"It is important to understand that when you are ready for the information, when you require an answer, it will make itself known to you. Watch, listen and trust. Sometimes the source will be from people or places you least expect. The critical element is the question. If you do not have the question you will not find the answer."

The clock began its ringing again. WAKE UP, WAKE UP! There was that smell again.

He picked up the book. The ringing stopped.

Duxter opened a page at random. To his surprise there

was something to read:

"When one takes a FUTURE FOCUS—PRESENT ACTION strategy, there is a gap between the current reality and the future state. It is natural and necessary. In fact, all gaps can be defined as 'life messes', personal barriers and strategic barriers."

He read on:

"Life Messes are those things in your life that create tension within you. You can tell they are messes if they have persisted in your life for some time but you have done nothing about them. When you think about them they sometimes put you in a bad mood. These require a decision to TAKE ACTION NOW!

"Personal Barriers are more attitudinal in nature. Limiting beliefs, feelings, habits, fears that you have and that are getting in the way of your success. Could be behaviours that are sabotaging you. These require a decision to TAKE ACTION NOW!"

"Strategic Barriers—those barriers that can be overcome with information.

Typically, we confuse these with personal barriers but this is erroneous. Strategic barriers are typically easy to deal with because they are more concrete in nature—money, education, skills, support, etc. These require a decision to **TAKE ACTION NOW!"**

"Ask the right question, you will find the information that you seek. Of course, you may not always like the answer, or accept it as the solution, but so be it.

"Close these gaps and you will reach your goals."

It went on...

"What is your goal, your future focus (state in the present tense)? What is the gap that exists between you and your goal? Therein lies the solution. What do you need to do to create the solution outcome (present action)?"

Duxter closed the book and thought about these questions. He thought back to his dream. His future focus was to be on the other side of the chasm. This he would accomplish by leaping over the chasm. The gap, he thought, was the gap (this, he thought was a strategic barrier, physical surroundings), the distance between one side of the chasm and the other. The solution was to jump it. For that to occur, he would need to be in better physical and mental shape. The present action—get into shape to make the leap.

Duxter was getting excited for the first time in a very long time. He could feel his passion for the future growing. He again opened the book to see what gifts it had to offer. Again something appeared. It listed out five simple but poignant statements.

The five reasons why we know we are ready to take the leap:

- we are ready to hear the message of our NIGGLE

- we believe that what we WANT is really what we WANT

- we believe we have the skill, talent or resources to achieve it

- we accept our desires and dreams as being legitimate

- it's TIME.

The Duxter Companion

Duxter laughed when he read the last reason. It was so obvious now.

Duxter now had the action plan he needed. He built up his stamina and leg strength. He noticed his attitude towards the State of Can't had changed, it was almost tolerant somehow. He now had a goal, something to overcome. He had, as the book said, a Future Focus. Oh, he did not accept the State of Can't, he merely knew how to cope with it until he could do something about it.

Of course, to reach his Future Focus would always require some challenges. Duxter included them in his strategy.

There was no point in waiting. He knew what he had to do.

Duxter Meets Up
With the Stranger

His first task was to go back to the chasm and estimate the distance from side to side. Back at his room, he practised the jump. At first he fell short by a considerable distance, and knew the goal was more difficult than first imagined. Over the weeks though, his jumps became longer and longer.

One day while he was practising outside at a park, where he had first met Will, I. Can't arrived to introduce himself. Duxter recognised him from the Christmas party.

"My how nice it is to finally meet you," I. Can't said, wringing his hands in delight. "I have waited a long time." He took Duxter's hand and shook it with excitement. "I do hope you are enjoying your stay with us."

"I must be frank," said Duxter. "I have already left U., and you."

"But I can't let you," I. Can't said. "You have chosen to be here and here you will stay. I know you will stay, won't you, Duxter." He could feel the pull of I's influence, the same power he'd felt at the party. And he could feel himself again becoming stuck, but struggled to break free.

"I... I... have already gone," he said, grabbing his knapsack, and running toward the hedge. The opening to Can was only twenty-five yards away, only a short distance of grass. A whistle blew. He looked behind and saw a group of T.S. police chasing him. If he could just make it to the hedge, he would disappear into the forest and be safe. As he ran, the group got nearer. They seemed to be able to run at great speeds. I. Can't was laughing. "You will never escape…"

Duxter looked behind at I. Can't and out of nowhere saw Will, the Bellhop, and a group of other rebels surrounding I.

"Go, Duxter!" his friends shouted. "You will make it this time! Go!"

He could feel the leaves of the hedge. The "They Say" police had stopped and turned around to help their Leader. Duxter went through the hedge and into the jungle. On and on he ran. He did not turn back.

Duxter made it to the chasm and stopped. He was breathless, panting so hard that he thought his chest would explode. He collapsed to the ground and sat for many minutes catching his breath. He noticed nothing but the silence. Peace wrapped itself around his body once more. He smiled. Had he been aware of it, he would have noticed the chattering monkeys had disappeared. He had been so caught up in his escape that he had ignored them, they had gone.

He looked up and noticed the sign…

A Leap of Faith Is Required

"So, they have taken my best people." Duxter turned around with a start. Coming through the trees was the Elder.

"I am sorry. It is my fault they have been captured." Duxter dropped his head. "I should have gone back to help them."

"What could you have done? You forget, my friend," she said while putting her hand on his shoulder, "that we have just won another victory. You have made it through. Protecting you was their choice. That is what personal responsibility is all about. Anyway, nothing will happen to them. I. Can't can't keep them, he knows as well as you that the struggle is based on having polarity. He will let them go soon enough. He does not have the energy to keep them."

"You mean I could have gone at any time? That I. Can't would have let me go?"

"He would have let you go and did so as soon as you chose to go. Duxter, surely you know things occur when they are supposed to. There is no 'If'—only 'Now' or 'Then.' Now is the time."

Duxter stood up and put on his knapsack. He was ready. "I am not sure if I can make the leap. I never found out if I can jump the distance." Again he saw the sign:

Faith Is Required

He opened his knapsack and taking out the companion turned to the following words:

Trust yourself!

You know exactly what you have to do.

Don't you?

The Duxter Companion

He took one final look across to the other side of the chasm. Briefly, a creature showed itself to Duxter. He knew instantly it was his possibility. It was tall and hairy and seemed to be audaciously taunting him to come over to try and catch him. It seemed to be laughing at Duxter's indecisiveness.

Duxter was shocked and somewhat taken aback at seeing his possibility so clearly, but also motivated to capture it. How dare it laugh at him. He thought. The possibility was the energy Duxter needed to make the leap he needed to accomplish. He took a deep breath and ran towards the edge. It came up at him faster and faster. Then he jumped into the void.

It was as though all of his experiences came together into one point as his feet left the ground. All he had learned over the course of his life was applied for this purpose; this one moment in time. He felt himself rising higher into the air. The limiting weight of his past fell away and he became light. Higher he rose, as if the support of all those people in his life who believed in him were lifting him over the chasm. He could hear the air whooshing by his ears just like in the dream. The wind blew through his hair. He could see the other side coming closer to him. He could feel the excitement of his success. Just as he had seen, it came true. In a flash, he was over.

The speed at which he reached his goal had startled him. He looked around to reasure himself, to confirm that truly, he had jumped. He saw the Elder smiling, on the other side of the chasm. She called across to him—

"Duxter! Remember! Remember us! We shall always be with you, even when you do not know it!"

"Thank you!" he shouted back.

"No, Duxter, we thank *you*," and she disappeared.

Somewhat dazed from his accomplishment, Duxter plunked himself on the ground to catch his breath. He took his companion from his knapsack and opened it, and without fail, a quote presented itself.

Until you can see the outcome in your mind,
it will be difficult to see it in reality.
The Duxter Companion

He chuckled to himself at what he had read as he slung his knapsack over his back. He stuffed the book into his pocket and he noticed a sign up ahead:

"Yes!" he yelled, throwing his arms in the air and dancing around. This was what he had wanted. Here he was. Unbeknownst to Duxter, far up ahead his possibility did a little jig.

More Secrets of the Knapsack

Duxter felt alive and energized. Jumping the chasm had given him back his passion. He felt young and invigorated. He opened up his knapsack and took out the *Companion* to see what it would have to say.

Your knapsack, as you have no doubt noticed, stores only the most important of things. Everything else will be discarded over time.

Duxter stopped to put the memory of his jump into his knapsack for safe-keeping. You see, Duxter had learned the value of storing experiences, especially successful ones. Experiences, he now knew, contained the resourceful information he could use at a later date.

"The beauty of storing this information in my knapsack," he finally said to himself, after reading the *Companion*, "is that you don't take it for granted. Every success is a worthy success and should be packed away for safe-keeping."

What he noticed was that, though he had travelled a great distance, his knapsack was neither too full nor too empty, neither too light nor too heavy. So the memory slipped easily into the pack. Now, when he stored that memory away, he discarded less useful thoughts. Thoughts that he had accumulated before he realized he was on a journey. Dark, foreboding thoughts that had begun to eat away at his knapsack, slowly, purposefully, and subtly.

His knapsack of course was full of all sorts of these

thoughts, for it would take some time to have all his dark thoughts of bad experiences dissolve into nothing—or would it?

He had just finished collecting his thoughts off the ground when he noticed something lying partly exposed under a bush. He walked over, and picked up a pair of glasses. Though he did not need glasses with which to see, he tried them on anyway.

"Huh," he said, unimpressed. "I can see as well as I could before."

Suddenly, out of the corner of his eye came a flash. He took the glasses off quickly, for he thought they would impede his sight, but he could not see it again. The flash did not repeat itself. His thoughts drifted away as quickly as the flash, so he stored the glasses in his pack.

After lunch, Duxter got under way once again. The going was easier and he gained a great deal of time.

As the going was easy, Duxter's mind went back to the glasses. He took his knapsack off his back and began to rummage around for them. Finally, he felt them at the very bottom where they had sunk while he walked.

He took the glasses out and put them on.

He looked back into the knapsack, and saw a large, dark, solid object sitting at the bottom where his glasses had been. He remembered when he had picked this bad experience up. The experience was not pleasant and had remained in his pack for some time. He had just not been able to get rid of it. He picked it out to mull it over and felt the weight of it in his hands.

With the glasses on things were different. Though it was heavy and dark, he could see the experience in a different light. Somehow the experience was clearer to him. He noticed that it contained bright, colourful and valuable gems of learnings. Looking closer into the colours, he decided to break the object into pieces. He would keep the bright colourful gems and discard the rest. He realised as he broke it up that the darker chunks began to crumble in his hands like sand flowing through his fingers.

He smiled as he stored the colourful learnings back in his knapsack, knowing now that the past experience had not been a failure after all.

He took the glasses off.

"Wow, it appears these glasses have given me an insight into my experiences that I hadn't noticed before. It allows me to reframe the experience," he exclaimed loudly, surprising himself at his own reaction.

Duxter felt lighter, the pack felt lighter and being the fine day it was this made sense to him.

As he continued on through the forest though he began to notice it was getting darker. It seemed unknown to him, foreign, as if he hadn't experienced this forest before (which of course he had not); the trees were taller, the underbrush thicker, the air cooler and he noticed the pungent smell of rotting leaves.

He became aware of his feelings and it was strange because he felt he should be afraid, at least he would have been before, but this time he walked on, confident that he would handle whatever came his way. He looked back into his knapsack and saw this time the experience of a little while back, when he had to follow Will Powers through what seemed to be an uncharted path, that they were creating as they went along. He looked at that experience and noticed that where before he had been afraid of the unknown, now it shone with intensity. It was actually beautiful. He again held the experience in his hand to see it fully. It was made up of bright, beautiful colors, of brilliant yellows, oranges, reds, and blues, each one representing a different resource he had used to make his way through to the rebel encampment, even if at the time he did not recognize having used any resources. He saw that in order to follow Will, he had to use energy, perseverance, creativity, and most of all a belief that the current situation was unacceptable. A belief that change was worth it. No matter how scared he was of the unknown he was better off choosing to go forward.

He looked at the colourful memory for some time. He felt the surge of energy rush through his body as it had then. He saw the expression of perseverance on his face, and he heard WILL POWERS relax him.

He looked at the forest he was about to enter. He now understood where his confidence came from.

He relaxed. He looked at the experience again and did not see how scared he once was, or that there had been times when he did not want to go on. He did not see those times because he had not put them in his knapsack. They had disappeared. Satisfied, he put the experience back in his knapsack, feeling that he was now ready to go into the dark unfamiliar part of the forest.

The Forest of Possibilities

He proceeded into the new experience.

Duxter moved through the forest. He knew that being on guard was alright because it allowed him to remain alert to possible problems. But he also knew that he had all the resources he needed in his knapsack so that he possessed confidence and had nothing to fear.

After a while he came across a shovel, stuck in the soft dirt. The shovel was a basic ordinary shovel with a short wood shaft, metal handle and shiny metal spade. It looked brand new. Attached to the handle was a note in big, bold, phosphorescent letters.

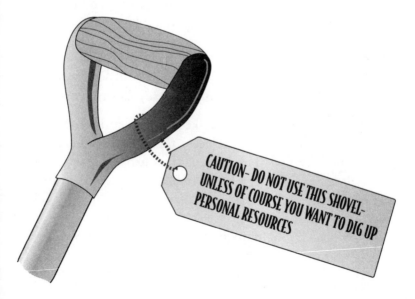

CAUTION- DO NOT USE THIS SHOVEL- UNLESS OF COURSE YOU WANT TO DIG UP PERSONAL RESOURCES

He pondered the meaning of the note for some time, curious as to any demand that forbade him from doing something. "Hmm…" A shovel that helped him dig up personal resources? Physical resources yes, gold, soft topsoil maybe, but qualities like energy, confidence, calm, patience, and other resources? This might be of assistance at some time. So he put the note in his pocket and the shovel in his pack and carried on toward his destination.

Duxter, as he travelled through the forest hour by hour, mile by mile, noticed little glimmers of light. The farther he travelled the more he noticed areas where the glimmers became fuller, rounder, brighter. He looked into the bright lights and noticed pleasant sights. These sights made him feel comfortable, at ease with his surroundings. "Am I getting used to the new experience?" he asked himself. "Or is it that these sights have always been there?" The shadows that he thought were strange and interesting began to take shape as wonderful exotic plants, age-old trees, and animals. He had a strange sense they were watching him as he progressed.

Possibilities travel by your door all day, every day.
All you need do is put your hand out and grab them.
The Duxter Companion

He pondered this as he walked on. He let the oneness of the forest surround him. He heard the forest breathe. In and out as he breathed. The ancient trees exhaled. He noticed himself feeling stronger, his head becoming clear and fresh. The air was clean. He inhaled, the forest inhaled. The rhythm was exhilarating.

"Notice life," he thought he heard it say. "Notice what is going on now," it whispered.

As he looked closer in the light, he began to notice possibilities. Possibilities that had not appeared to him when he was anxious. It seemed to him the forest began to open up to him when he let go of protecting himself from it. He felt the sense of a path under his feet, the rustle of the leaves above his head, and the smell of rotting leaves became the smell of life giving back to itself.

As he transcended his own being and opened up to the forest, when he focused outside himself, he began to notice opportunities of beauty, opportunities of the sounds of life and opportunities from the feeling of connectedness he had with the forest. He noticed the possibility he was pursuing duck behind a tree. He also noticed the stream ahead. He decided to stop to rest. He hoped his possibility would wait for him.

He sat down by the brook and cupped his hands to take a cool refreshing drink. As he dipped his hands into the water he was aware of its cold intensity. His whole body became fresh and alive. He noticed his face as the water became still. He was bathed in energy. Though he was still a body, he seemed to be more than just his mass. He was an intensity. The forest was attracted to him, the plants were calling for him and though he hadn't noticed it yet a chipmunk sat next to him. Duxter jumped at the sight of his unexpected visitor.

Rather than scurrying away, the chipmunk stared at him. Duxter was mesmerized by the animal. "Welcome to the forest," it seemed to be saying. "Do not be afraid, we cannot hurt you."

Duxter chuckled at the irony of the statement coming from a chipmunk. "I have been asked to approach you because of my size. Others, like the bear, wanted to come but we felt you might not understand our motives."

Duxter smiled understanding and thanked the animal for its kindness.

"How is it possible that I can understand you?" querried Duxter.

"Why do you believe that you can suddenly understand me?"

"I do not understand. I know what you say to me, yet clearly you are not making sounds, but I do know that we are communicating."

"So, I ask you again," countered the chipmunk, "why do you believe that now? This forest was created because it was possible to create. Life is possibility and so we are talking now. We have always had that possibility, though not in the way you believe it to be. Even now we are not talking as you would to a friend, but we are talking just the same. You humans, you're so dense, we communicate with you every day. When tens of thousands of birds use to darken the sky during a migration, now only hundreds might be seen today. This is communicating something. We are all connected, what happens to us happens to you eventually."

Suddenly there was a roar from right behind them. Duxter jumped.

"Okay, okay," shouted the chipmunk. "I'll stay on topic, geez keep your fur on!"

Duxter quickly looked around "What was all that about?"

"That was the bear blustering on like he always does when he doesn't get his way. He was afraid I was going to start lecturing you. I'm sort of an opinionated little guy." The chipmunk looked back at the bear and signaled to be quiet.

"Oh," laughed Duxter with relief, "I thought I was tonight's dinner. The chipmunk rolled his eyes. "It's interesting," Duxter continued, changing topics, "that we should be talking about possibility. I have always believed that possibility offers only once. That if you don't grab it then, it is gone forever. Yet, just before sitting down, I saw it all around me in the forest."

"We, in nature, certainly believe that. When a wolf hunts a deer, it does not believe that the deer it did not catch is the only deer it could ever catch. It merely seeks another deer. It does not become disappointed or angry at itself for missing an opportunity. It merely waits for the possibility to exist again. It passes no judgment. Mother Nature passes no judgment. Why do you?"

"But there are times when I feel desperate that if I don't reach the goal then I have missed my chance. I will be too old. It will be too late."

"The wolf would argue, if it were here, that it was not meant to be this time. It knows that it cannot catch every animal in its sights. But it continues to try regardless of its age or physical capacities. The forest is possibility. Life is possibility." Duxter paused to think about this.

"What if I never get what I want?" he responded.

"Wait a minute. Never? Do you really believe that to be true?" The chipmunk giggled. "How can that be if life is possibility created? Look around you Duxter, the forest surrounds you with proof."

Duxter paused, "Okay, let me for a minute agree that life is possibility. That would mean that I don't even have to try? That is not how I was brought up. I was taught to try hard, sweat, and bleed if you have to. You're saying watch for the opportunities that arise and go after them then."

"That's correct. Just watch for the opportunity and go after it."

"If life is possibility," Duxter continued, "I took that to mean that there is an abundance of life. So, if there is abundance, then maybe I don't have to try, it will just show up."

"Try? No, do not try. Decide to do, but do not try. Trying

has no commitment. It is merely an attempt, a half hearted attempt at best. You can decide not to act. This would be fine. You can also decide to act. But if this is your decision, then so be it, act. In fact, as soon as you decide to act give it your best. But I want to make a distinction for you. Being committed to your goal is not the same thing as being emotionally attached. The wolf is not emotionally attached to the outcome. He is also highly aware of the present and of its offerings and is able to take advantage of them. That is the difference. There is a deep knowing in nature. This knowing is a very powerful presence in all of us."

"What is it that you know?" asked Duxter.

"The knowing is an intense peace. A peace so deep it contains an unquestioning belief that what you seek you will receive. We are never sure humans truly understand this exists within them but let me help you uncover this truth with a question. Listen very carefully. If you absolutely knew that no matter what happened you would be fine, what would be possible? How would you feel?"

Duxter thought about the deepest meaning of this question. "Anything would be possible. I would fear nothing. I would worry about nothing. I would just know that I would do it. There would be no need to think anything but act. I would know that I could handle any situation that was presented. Any challenge that was put in my way I would overcome." He stopped and looked down into the stream.

He saw his own reflection and he laughed. "I would be at peace about the future."

"That Duxter, is the knowing. We know life is possibility. We have no fear about the future, or the past."

Silence filled the space and Duxter looked over at his new friend. "This is what you have been trying to tell us?"

The chipmunk seemed agitated by the question and

laughed. "Duxter, we have been trying to tell you for thousands of years." He suddenly changed his attitude, paused, and sighed. "But it doesn't matter how long it takes to understand, just as long as eventually you do." Another minute passed between them. "I must be going now. I have dinner to collect. Goodbye, my friend." The chipmunk scurried off behind a tree. Duxter picked up his knapsack and left. His mind couldn't shake the conversation. It was as if he was in sort of a trance. "Knowing, knowing, knowing. Yes." He felt the forest breathe.

Duxter Discovers How Time Works

As the forest became lighter for him he noticed a cottage, off in the distance, through the trees. So he veered off his path, following one that presented itself and headed towards the cottage. He noticed that it was very old, a white stucco building, framed by thick logs and a slate roof. Smoke billowed from the chimney. Someone was home.

He approached the cottage and saw an ornate sign on the front door:

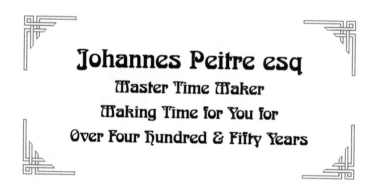

Johannes Peitre esq
Master Time Maker
Making Time for You for
Over Four Hundred & Fifty Years

Duxter knocked on the door, which was slightly ajar. It opened slowly. He peered inside. A very old Clock was crouched over a large wooden table, looking through a watchmaker's eyepiece. It seemed absorbed in its task. Duxter was not sure if he had been noticed. The Time Maker had not looked up.

"Good afternoon. Please have a seat," it said. "I will be with you in a moment."

Duxter looked around the shop. On the table next to him, lay the latest copy of the IN TIME Journal. Duxter leafed through it and saw articles and advertisements outlining the latest methods and tools used in the trade. The articles listed on the cover included, "Time waits for no one—ten ways of catching up to it." Johannes Peitre himself had written a piece entitled, "What time is it really?—Zen and the art of keeping time." Duxter was impressed.

On all the walls hung timepieces. Large old clocks with huge faces, small ornate ones, ones in need of repair, some yet to be completed, and beautiful new ones with smaller hands and unblemished faces not yet ravished by time.

"What can I do for you, young man?"

Duxter was not young but he was certainly not as old as this clock who, if the sign was right, must be over four hundred or so years of age. Anyone would be younger than that.

"Is there a piece you like?"

"Forgive me, I have never talked to a clock before."

"You are forgiven for that oversight," it said, smiling.

"I am merely travelling through. I hope I am not intruding."

"Not at all. I make time for everyone," it said, chuckling at its own humour. "Please, let me show you around." The clock came around the table. "Can I get you some tea, or lunch perhaps?"

"Tea would be fine." The clock was gone for many minutes and returned with a tea trolley.

"I was noticing that all the clocks are noted by levels. Level 1, Level 2, Level 3, Level 4 and so on."

"Yes, and do you notice the hands, how they move?" Duxter got up to take a closer look. He went to the only clock not classified by a number.

"In fact, the clock I am seeing has no hands. I cannot even tell what time it is."

"Ah, yes," said the Clock, fixing the tea on the tray. "You are looking at a very, very young clock. A clock of this age is a pre-apprentice and has yet to grasp even an awareness of time. It will though, with experience and training. You see," the Clock continued, "it does not know that it does not know and therefore lives completely in Bliss and so has no need for hands. For it, the only time is the present. The apprenticeship will start for this clock shortly and go on for as long as it takes."

"An apprenticeship?"

"Yes. All clocks go through an apprenticeship. They must understand how time works. Many are on time. A few are out of time. Only those that reach a state of being 'in time' will be allowed to go on."

Duxter followed the clocks around the wall. His eyes fell upon a clock that seemed to be out of control. Its hands were moving backward and forward, sometimes not moving at all. Sometimes it was keeping time, sometimes rushing time and sometimes slowing time down to a crawl. Johannes, who had gone back to the worktable, looked up from a timepiece it was working on. "Ah, yes, I have yet to be able to rectify these ones as they go through this stage of their growth," it said, dropping its work and coming to stand beside Duxter. "My only observation is, clocks go through a particularly difficult time at this stage in their development. They are aware of time but do not, as yet, know how to control it. They do much experimenting and you are now seeing the results of that experimentation. This is what I call the 'they know that they do not know' period. It can be very frustrating for them."

But he laughed as a wise but patient teacher might at a pupil who has made a significant but wrong discovery. "The real challenges are those who 'think they know what they do not know'. Ah, but they are impetuous. Making many mistakes and making many discoveries. All that I can do is let them find out for themselves and be there when they are ready to listen."

Duxter smiled. He was thinking of his own children. "How long did it take this clock to reach level two?"

"For this clock, fifteen years, although each will do it at its own time," said the master, holding the clock in his hand and lovingly stroking it, as Duxter might his own daughter's hair.

"This training takes many years," responded Duxter. "I mean, this clock has been on the wall for fifteen years and has yet to learn all there is to time and being a clock. I don't know if I could be that patient," laughed Duxter.

"Ah, well, I am not sure if it is patient. It lets me know in no uncertain terms that it feels ready to go out into the world." Johannes smiled. "Being a master timepiece takes great skill and knowledge," the old clock went on. "And clocks must reach the mastery level before they can leave here. Think about how significant time is to you. Virtually everything you do, your whole life in fact, revolves around time. When a clock is ready, you will be running your life by it. They must fully understand time for you, to be as effective as you need to be. They have a very important role to play and they take this responsibility very seriously."

Duxter thought back to the alarm clock in his knapsack, how it had helped him.

"I must sit for a while." The old clock started to pour the steeped tea.

Duxter moved along the wall to a Level Three clock.

"That one has been here for twenty-five years," said the master, handing Duxter the tea.

Duxter noticed that this clock seemed to be more in control of itself. The hands were moving slowly but consistently around the face of the clock.

"This clock," said the master, "is still in the learning period of understanding. It is beginning to be aware of its competence and so can control itself, but has yet to understand. You see, a clock expresses its feelings through its hands. This clock's hands are moving slowly because it feels that it is taking too much time to become a master timepiece. It is entering the time paradox. It has the time to learn but does not want to take the time. It is at this point when some clocks do not make it. They become too impatient, not prepared to put in the effort and energy necessary for mastery."

"What happens to them?"

" I must put them at the back of the shop and start the process over with them. They will understand eventually."

"When does mastery occur?"

"For a clock, mastery occurs when it becomes unconscious of its ability to keep accurate time. Its hands move around the dial with simplicity and effortlessness. I know that this stage is reached when I can look at the clock and be unaware that the hands are moving at all, yet know that time is being accurately measured just the same. In short, I know what time it is,"said the master, smiling.

Duxter laughed.

"What is time really, Duxter? Over the span of a lifetime, a month, a year is of little concern. What makes it of concern is one's perception or feelings of what is happening at any one moment. If one is experiencing difficulties or change, that same year can feel like an eternity. A clock that is challenged, will need to take a wide perspective on its development and learn to be patient, knowing that it has the whole rest of its life to be a clock."

"Yet that wide perception, as you call it, is very difficult to keep," Duxter responded. "I mean, while you are going through it, you feel like it will go on forever. How do your clocks keep that wide perspective?"

"I teach them how to look at themselves from outside their point of development and to see their entire lives. They see how much time they really do have left and how much they have accomplished over that time. I must say right here that it doesn't mean they become unwilling to work toward mastery, as if they had all the time in the world, it just helps them to separate the unproductive emotions from the reality. When they can do that, they are able to put their training into perspective. They learn to take what we call a 'whole lifetime perspective'. Did you notice, Duxter, that no clock here has a sweep second hand?"

Duxter looked more closely. "Hm. Yes."

"No clock," the master went on, "will get a sweep second hand until it can master time without it. Then it will receive the sweep second hand as an honour and graduation recognition."

"What about this clock?" Duxter looked at a Level Four clock. Its hands were moving much faster.

"This clock is at the other end of the time paradox. For it, time is moving faster, or so it feels anyway, so the hands move around the face faster, demonstrating its fear that it will run out of time. Yet, when it reaches this stage, most clocks will take the time necessary to learn their craft. One or two more years, more or less, will make no difference. It has already taken the time. It knows that when it has mastered time, it will have many more years of productive life.

It has more patience and understanding of how mastery and life works. It is close to completing its learning. In fact, this one will slow itself down any day now and keep time like the true master I know it is. I expect great things from this one."

"Is it finally understanding whole lifetime perspective?" asked Duxter.

"Clocks reach mastery at different times," responded the master. "For some it is reached earlier, for others, later. It makes no difference. You will still be able to use it effectively."

"This is quite a shop you have here," said Duxter.

"Thank you. Well, you might be interested in knowing, that we started to look into working with calendars, but I find them so one-dimensional and quite regimented."

Duxter laughed as he sat down to finish his tea. He looked over at the old clock who was resting his eyes. Duxter wondered how long had it taken the old clock to become a master. He thought about his own development and how he might be able to make some changes relatively quickly, but it might require a little time and focus to make others. And when he really thought about it, all the clocks reached mastery at different times, depending on the natural flow of their own development. They couldn't push time nor could they slow time down. Was life not like that anyway? It just was. He might have to accept that the solution to his filling in the gap (the clarity of his purpose) would happen when it happened.

Like the forest, he would watch and listen for it.

The clock was snoring in the chair, its head bobbing back and forth. Duxter wrote a note of thanks and left the cottage. He stored his new insight and experience in his knapsack. Another, less useful, experience from his past disappeared.

We Should Do Lunch

Through the trees up ahead, Duxter noticed what looked like a clearing. There was an open field that seemed to go on for many miles. Over in the distance was a mountain range, its snow-capped peaks glistening in the sunshine. It had been a long time since he had seen a sun so bright, so vibrant, so life-giving. He stopped to enjoy the rays, and to reflect upon the warmth. The sun felt warm on his face. With his hands tucked under his head, and his legs crossed in front of him, he lay on his back chewing on a long strand of hay.

He hadn't realized he'd fallen asleep but when he awoke it struck him that he hadn't seen his possibility for a while. He looked around the open field but it was nowhere in sight. It seemed to have vanished. He knew that it was time to move ahead so, with his focus on the distant mountains, he started to walk. At first he was worried he would not see his possibility ever again, but his conversation with the chipmunk came back to him. He had nothing to fear. He would catch his possibility when the time was right.

The day continued to be bright. Not a cloud to be found in the sky. Up in the near distance to his left, he saw what looked like a very high pole with a platform attached. There seemed to be a lump on top of the platform. He went to investigate. As he got closer, the shape started to take form. At first he thought it was a pile of rocks, then a pile of clothes, until finally he saw that it was a human form, and it seemed to be studying the sky very attentively.

By the time the sun was high in the sky, Duxter reached the base of the pole.

He shielded his eyes from the sun and yelled to the person.

"Excuse me!... Uh... Hm..." Duxter cleared his throat.

"Yes? Can't you see I am busy? Go away and do not disturb me! I am studying the formation flying yonder."

Duxter looked ahead into the sky but could only see what looked like a line of birds in a classic "V" formation.

"You are studying those geese?"

"Yes, now please be quiet!"

Some time passed.

"You are still here?"

"Well I only wanted to..."

"Oh, if you insist on bothering me, come up the pole and do try to be quiet."

A basket came down the pole. Duxter hopped in and propelled himself up the pole.

At the top, Duxter had quite a view. His eye caught a group of what looked like little prairie dogs, running in circles.

"Could you tell me what those creatures over yonder might be?"

"Please don't bother me with trivialities. I am a professor studying the 'Shoulds' and they are coming our way. Though they are plentiful, it is not often one really gets to study their habits. I come here every year to do field work."

"Excuse me Professor, I did not realise your work was so important."

The 'shoulds' flew closer. Duxter could hear their discussion, "Should we land here?" asked one. "Oh yes, we should," honked another. "But maybe there would be better," honked yet another.

"You will notice their speech pattern and how it affects their behaviour. They seem unable or unwilling to commit to a decision. How extraordinary," exclaimed the professor with glee. "Every year they migrate from the state of Should to the state of Won't via Someplace Else. What is interesting is that they alway land in exactly the same spot, yet have never once agreed to it." The birds swooshed overhead, the sound of their wings creating a hiss as they flew by.

They landed, but as the professor had predicted, on a spot none could agree on.

Duxter heard one of the group yell out, "We should have landed there instead."

"Let us go down and make a closer observation." Taking his note pad and tape recorder, the professor pushed by Duxter. "Well are you coming or not?" Duxter jumped into the basket.

The birds were very large, standing perhaps four feet from head to toe, their wing span about six feet or more. They seemed to know the professor and were quite polite.

"Good afternoon Professor, it is so nice to see you again." they agreed. "Have you brought an assistant this year?"

"This is... I am afraid I do not know your name."

"I'm Duxter Hexter," said Duxter, smiling and putting his hand out to shake the wing of the bird, but then thinking better of it.

What a curious name, thought the professor, to himself.

"Well it is very nice to make your acquaintance, I'm sure," replied the birds in unison. "The Professor has been studying us for three years now, is that not right Professor?"

"Why, yes. Has it been that long? My theory is that the way these birds communicate affects their flight pattern. You see, word patterns reflect their beliefs and beliefs of course get reflected in their behaviour. There is then a circular relation, each reinforcing the other. The Should birds use of the word 'should' merely reflects a difficulty in making decisions. Several factors may cause this circularity of action. Lack of self worth, lack of standards, inability to make commitment, or perhaps they simply do not have the confidence to make a decision on where to land. They may be too afraid of offending each other. Who knows really, but that is one of the reasons why I am studying them."

The birds looked at the professor as if he was from another planet.

The professor went on to say that if the birds understood these connections, they would be able to make decisions, whether right or wrong, agreed to or not by the other members of the flock. They would also not procrastinate or behave in a tentative manner when decisions needed to be made.

"He explains this to us every year and we still don't know what he's talking about. What does he say we can do to get over this?" laughed one of the birds.

"Oh yes, add three words to the end of each 'should',— 'BUT I WONT'." They found this so funny that many of them were rolling on the ground in a fit of laughter.

"Oh, Professor, you do crack us up!"

The professor looked disgusted with them. "What I mean is that these three words, 'BUT I WON'T', when added to the end of a 'should' sentence, create a tension within the speaker that forces him to reflect upon whether what he said is truly what he wants to do. This then gives him free choice to act or not.

"For instance, let us say that I need to go to the doctor and I say to you, 'I should go to the doctor this afternoon.' This reflects the fact that I know I need to go but do not really want to. But, if I say, 'I should go to the doctor this afternoon… but I won't', then all of a sudden I am making a decision. Then I can ask myself, is this a correct decision or not? Understand?"

Duxter did. He knew that many times he would not be completely truthful with himself or others when he used the word "should".

"There are many words that reflect our beliefs," said the professor.

Duxter knew first hand of two—"I can't,'" but there were are others like,—"I never get what I want",—"that's just the way it is, that's just me",—"that's impossible,"—"well, it's Monday,"—or, "I just got out on the wrong side of the bed today."

"Ya, Okay, whatever, Professor," responded the flock.

For the rest of the afternoon the professor met with various birds, taking notes and recording their speech patterns. Finally they ignored him as they began to feed and rest in preparation for the remainder of their journey.

Suddenly, they began to form into their flight pattern. "Well, Professor, as usual it has been good to see you. We hope your studies are worthwhile but, for the life of us, we do not completely understand what you are doing studying a flock of birds. It has been, as always, a pleasure." Turning to Duxter, "It was nice meeting you Duxter." They tipped their wings and were off.

"We should do lunch sometime!" one of them yelled back to the professor.

"What a great idea!" exclaimed the rest of the flock and then they were gone.

"They say that every year and yet have never done it," remarked the professor, shaking his head. "Well, Duxter, it's time for me to get back to the university and write my paper. It has truly been a pleasure spending time with you." He paused in thought. "I find this study stimulating but occasionally lonely. I shall not say that we should meet back here again, but if you are in the neighbourhood, here is my card. Goodbye."

And the professor headed off toward the western horizon.

Duxter thought about that meeting. Maybe the professor was onto something there.

Hmm. He decided to become aware of his own speech patterns and notice how he acted. He stored the learning in his knapsack for future reference.

His mind went back to the creatures he had seen going around in circles. "Oh, Professor... wait! Could you tell me about...?" But the professor was by then too far away to hear.

Duxter Encounters the Yabut

The Duxter *Companion* defines a "YABUT" as follows—

"The YABUT is a closed-minded little creature that is afraid to listen. It is more interested in hearing its own voice, and in discussing its own troubles, than in hearing what others have to say. When approaching a yabut, do so cautiously. Stay friendly, but non-committal. Give it plenty of room to go in circles. Engage this creature with great care." The Companion goes on to say—"If you do engage a Yabut by accident or are bitten by one, watch for the following signs:

A change in language, with a noticeable use of 'Ya But' whenever someone suggests something that just might solve your problem.

A visible stiffening of the body, usually around the shoulders and occasionally in the face.

Eyes that do not keep contact.

In addition to these signs, watch for a mind that begins to close to ideas and opportunities.

If you or someone close to you should show any of these signs, seek help immediately. But do not expect the affected to take advice. Should you wish to catch a Yabut, no trap will be effective. Great concentration and awareness of its presence is required. The only remedies, once bitten, are—

1) to be aware of the signs;

2) to have someone tell you they see those signs in you;

3) to accept that the others are trying to help, and

4) to change the habit."

Duxter, as of yet, had not read his *Companion* on the subject of the Yabut but he would, and then he would know what to do. For now though, he just continued walking. Ahead in the distance he noticed hundreds of little creatures almost like prairie dogs or ground hogs, some sticking up from their burrows, others running around in circles as if they were chasing their tails.

The closer he got, the louder they became. "Yabut, yabut, yabut!" they whined.

Duxter was quite taken aback. He opened his *Companion*, hoping it might provide an answer. It did. He chuckled.

Duxter started walking through them. The whining became louder, almost unbearable, as they conversed amongst themselves, discussing how hard life was, how unfair it all was. Duxter smiled and acknowledged them but kept his mouth shut.

Boy, it was hard not to say something, but he remembered the cautionary advice.

"Engage the creature with great care." He walked on unscathed. He had again learned an important lesson.

Sometimes it is best not to engage others.
The Duxter Companion

Duxter in a Fog

Duxter continued on his way closer to the mountains. Their peaks became higher and were clearly very steep. Just after dinner he reached the foothills and the base of one of the mountains. Now. believe it nor not, there in front of his nose was a sign.

LOOK FOR THE SIMPLICITY IN EVERYTHING.
YOU MAY EITHER CLIMB TO THE PEAK TO SAY YOU
HAVE DONE IT OR YOU MAY TAKE THE LIFT.

THE CHOICE IS YOURS!

He chose the lift.

Eventually he found it and walked in. He looked around the old elevator and saw beautiful brass fittings, a half-circle floor indicator with a large brass arrow and dial. The door was heavy and thick, engraved with a bas-relief of the mountain range, with a sun shining over the peaks. A heavy accordion gate covered the door. It was something he had seen in very old buildings of long ago.

He pressed the button that said SUMMIT. "I might as well go all the way to the top if I'm going to go," he said to himself. He looked at the ascending numbers.

It wasn't too long before he came to a sudden stop. The door opened and he walked out into cloud cover. He was mildly disappointed at not being able to see the view, particularly because he wanted to see where he had been— the city state of Can't, the plains, the desert of Nowhere. But he was only mildly disappointed. Had he really known why he was there his disappointment would have been far greater. He found himself unsure of which direction to go. He opened his *Companion*—

**Let go. Stop.
Breathe deeply and let your mind be still.
PEACE. The answer will come.**

He stopped in his tracks. The answer did come. Over in the near distance, he heard a voice. He moved towards it as if he were floating.

Being still was getting easier for him to do. But still uncomfortable. The rush, rush of daily life had always seemed more important than stopping. But up here it seemed so easy, as if it was becoming second nature.

"You have felt stillness?" Because of the cloud, the voice was coming from every direction and no particular direction. Duxter went back to when he was a child, walking with his father through the woods. The peace, security, and warmth came flooding back. He could almost feel his father's great hand surround his own once more.

"I... I... I... I have felt something I have not felt for a great many years. How can this be? I had all but forgotten."

"It is not surprising. It has always been with you but you have been caught up with life and yet life is more than just the day to day grind. Do you recall the forest breathing?"

"Why, yes."

"That is life too. In it are the answers and the questions. Come this way, Duxter."

He still could not see beyond the tip of his outstretched hand, but he let the stillness guide him.

In front of him sat a very young child, so very young he could have been Duxter's son.

"But you are so young," cried Duxter.

"And your concern with this is?"

"Well, I was expecting an old mystic, someone with a long beard, and rags. You are dressed in fine robes and sandals."

"I can take many forms or no form at all," responded the child. "You see me as a child because that is how you need to see me, even though you were expecting to see an old man."

"Who… who are you?" Duxter asked tentatively.

"I am 'The Heart of the Matter'. When you see me, you see all that you are and all that you know."

"Then I do not know too much, for you are young enough to be my son." Duxter sounded disappointed.

"Can you not learn from the young? Do not your own children teach you something about yourself and about life every day?"

Duxter reflected on this. He had been so caught up with things lately he could not remember the last time he had actually sat down with his children, let alone talked with them, except to scold them or to tell them what they could not do. He suddenly laughed aloud, a hearty belly laugh. It was almost a release. He recalled his conversations with U. Can't. He was no different.

"What is the matter Duxter?"

"Oh, nothing. I was just thinking. It's just that… Well, I don't always believe in my own children. My mind went back to how I played with my own children. How I tried to limit them." He thought back to actually playing with his children when they were young. He saw discomfort, and impatience, he saw himself trying to influence the play by trying to get his daughter to do it the right way instead of her way. Her way may not have been right from the adult perspective but was perfectly acceptable to her. He was afraid of playing the game outside its intended use. How childish he had been. He realized that to play as a child would require him to suspend his impatience and his ego. He had never really tried that before.

"But why do I need to see a child?" Duxter asked.

"Remember," replied the child, "I am 'The Heart of the Matter'."

Duxter Learns of Higher Order, of Purpose and of Sacrifice

"You have a very selfish perspective, Duxter. It is never 'we' or 'us'. You speak of 'I want', 'I this', 'I that'. The 'I' is impatient for gratification now, as is a child. So I show myself to you as a child." He paused. "Have you considered the ego, the 'I'? You believe erroneously that the ego is the heart of the matter. But this is not so."

The child began drawing several crude concentric circles in the dirt. The middle one he labeled 'I'. "This is the 'I' sphere," he pointed out. "It is the smallest because it is a small and limiting sphere. Here, all decisions are made with the 'I' in mind, not necessarily what is good for the 'we'. The 'I' creates a society of poor decisions with no perspective on the long-term impact for 'self' or 'us'."

"I am sorry. I don't understand the difference between the self and the ' I '," Duxter said.

"The self is who you are. It is your identity, personality, skills, values, strengths and everything else that makes up who you are. The 'I' is the part of you that thinks only of you, your needs and wants. It is interested in satisfying only a part of your self."

"That is a very fine distinction," exclaimed Duxter. "I mean, what I want is good for the self."

"That is not true and it is very easy to prove. As a child, if you remember, you ate five large chocolate bars at one sitting. The 'I' was very satisfied but you ended up getting very ill. Do you remember?"

"Yes," responded Duxter sheepishly. "I was sick for the rest of day and had to leave the summer fairgrounds and all my friends."

"How did that satisfy you?"

"It didn't. I had saved up all summer for that day and I wasted it in the first hour."

"The 'I' wanted to show off. The self wanted to stay and have fun. That is the distinction."

"Yes, I see. I shall satisfy myself when I focus on what the 'self'requires."

"The self needs to be challenged and stimulated," responded the child, "to prove that it can do what it says it can do. The 'I' is worried about looking good, sounding smart, not making mistakes and because this is so, you will limit your actions and possibility to satisfy the 'I'. That is the center of the circle. The self is what is left when all the masks are taken off. It is the authentic you," he said, pointing to Duxter. "The authentic you, the self, wants to be respected and honored. It wants to be loved and to love. It is you at your most powerful and joyful." The child continued on. "As we move out from the center we move to the family sphere. If you did nothing more than live honorably in this sphere you would have lived a satisfying life. As we move out to the far reaches of the circles we move right to humankind. This is the most difficult of climbs to make as it requires the greatest of sacrifice and a drive that stretches all possibility. You are not required to go there if you do not want to."

"This is all well and fine but what about the need for happiness?"asked Duxter. "If I am not happy, does that not affect how my family will be? Will they be happy?"

"Ah, yes happiness. I have heard a lot about the need for happiness. Happiness is argued by those of the 'I' sphere. The problem with happiness is that it is fleeting. It is like the honeymoon of a newlywed couple. Great while it lasts but really does not reflect the hard work and sacrifice required for a lifetime of commitment and satisfaction. The self, the true heart of the matter, is not interested in just happiness—it wants you to be your highest self, irrespective of how you may *feel* at the moment."

Duxter struggled with himself. "But am I not my highest self when I seek happiness?" Duxter was struggling with this idea. It was contrary to what he had always believed.

The child stopped and stared at Duxter with a look of disappointment spread over his face.

"What?" shouted Duxter.

"Remember what I said, Duxter. The self wants to be respected and honoured. It wants to love and be loved. It is you at your most powerful and joyful. It cannot attain this if you flit from one experience to the next, defining success by how happy it made you feel. You will remain incomplete and dissatisfied, always hoping that the next experience will give you what you seek."

Duxter was about to defend himself.

"Sit and be quiet," said the child. "Think about what you just heard." The child closed his eyes. Duxter remembered the quote in his *Companion*.

Let go. Stop.
Breathe deeply and let your mind be still.
PEACE. The answer will come.

He quieted his mind down and felt it empty. He started to really go beyond his 'I' need and stared deeply into the child. He began to see himself at the heart of the matter. He saw within the child power but not force. He began to see himself at his most powerful. He saw a strong sense of who he was as a person. He saw as he went deep into the heart of the matter what it would be like to be able to say "yes" or "no" to someone without discomfort. For others to know that, if he said he was going to do something, it was going to happen. No one would doubt his credibility. He would walk his talk. He saw that what was required from him was a higher set of terms. He needed to define what was acceptable and what was not.

He then and there decided to build a set of standards or terms by which he would live his life.

The first he decided would be, "My actions determine what I truly believe about something." He would then be required to think through a decision before he committed to it. Just saying it would not be enough.

The next he decided would be to treat others with respect by being clear with people. A "yes" would mean "yes", a "no" would mean "no". He would have to be up front with people, no more hiding behind his feelings, fears or other reactions.

Finally, he would accept responsibility for the choices he had made thus far and would make in the future. That meant that he had free will to create his life and decide to do nothing or do something.

The child looked over and smiled.

Duxter smiled back.

The child changed, his voice became almost a whisper. "You are now ready to participate in why you are really here. Come—sit here Duxter," he said.

Duxter sat closer to the child. He felt a strong connection with the child, with the mountain.

"If you looked over your life as if you were floating way above it..." Duxter found himself becoming more relaxed the longer he listened to the child's voice. "If you had a chance to..."

The rhythm of the child's voice was soothing. Before long, Duxter found himself drifting above the landscape until he saw the entire land below. Higher, until he saw his life in its entirety. He saw specific events from his past to his present, but only light and shadows, hills and valleys from his future. He continued to drift higher until he saw the entire world, then space. He wasn't afraid of what he saw. He drifted into the emptiness of the universe until he saw the earth as it really was, filled with billions and billions of interconnected beings, floating in a universe of space. How, he thought to himself, can we not be connected if we are the only living beings in the whole universe? How can we allow ourselves to be so separated from one another? How can we be so cruel?

He again heard the child's voice. "As you are floating, you will notice events and experiences from your life."

It was, in fact, Duxter's future that he saw. What was in store? Higher purpose?

He thought of his discoveries and what he had defined for his life and found that he could place it in his picture. Some things he saw could happen relatively soon, others would take much longer, even many years.

"You will see variety, times of great joy, sacrifice, happiness, and all the other things that life brings us. Perhaps years of one quality and then years of another."

Yes, Duxter did see that.

"But when all is said and done, happiness is just one of the qualities."

Yes, that was true.

"There are many ways to describe life. It can be interpreted as a continuous journey in which we are travellers, knowing our next destination, and often times anticipating the challenges we will face along the way, but more often than not facing them at the time. But perhaps you see it as a process of development and growth. Or it could be like a book, with a series of chapters, some ending, some beginning. Or it can be seen as a continuous link of experiences that only has real meaning at the end. Still it could be seen as a creation."

"A creation?"asked Duxter in a far away voice.

"Yes. We all build or design our lives. Some choose to create a life that is safe, limited and small."

Yes, Duxter could relate to that one. He smiled.

"Others choose to create something large and expansive. Neither is right or wrong, good or bad. They just are. What is important is what we choose to do with what life provides for us. We are like architects. When something happens to us that shakes us to the foundation, a loss of some sort, a problem or challenge, as architects we can design our reaction to that event. We can choose to let the event change us. We can get angry, feel like a victim and blame whatever circumstance or whomever to make us feel better again. This would be acceptable if this was what you want to create, if that is the part you choose to show the world. You would also be correct if you want to show your 'self' to the world. You have free will. Duxter, when you decided to become aware of your situation and realized you were nowhere, you also realized you were somewhere. That somewhere was unacceptable to you, so you created a journey that led you to me. That awareness provided you with options. With options we can create.

"Wait a minute." Duxter put his hand up to stop the child. "This journey was created to lead me to you?"

The child was smiling. "I am at the heart, the deepest

part of you. All the distance you have travelled, the challenges you have overcome, the experiences you have stored in your knapsack, all of it was to connect us. Duxter, what did the advertisement in the newspaper say? 'Visit places you have not been to in a while...'"

"But I thought the Can't brothers sent me that message!" exclaimed Duxter.

"They did. But that doesn't mean they didn't play a role in bringing us together. It is all part of the journey you created." There was a pause. Duxter let out a deep breath and snapped out of the state the child had put him in. He was truly back.

"Duxter, now that you have found me I will never leave you. So it is time for you to continue on your way. We have finished talking for now. You will not see me in this or any form other than you, ever again."

"Wait! I still don't understand how this journey was to lead me to you. I mean I understand that I created this journey but how could it be that I designed it to meet you? I didn't really know you existed."

"Do you recall your meeting with the master time maker?" asked the child.

Duxter nodded.

"During your conversation he told you of the clocks that do not even have an awareness of time. He described it as if it does not know that it does not know. You were like that clock. You did not know that I even existed, yet that does not mean I did not. I am after all the truest form of you. It just means you had no awareness of who you really are and what you really want. But you see, Duxter, I couldn't stay silent. Forever you have been seeking me, and every once in a while you would hear my calls. When you did listen, albeit for brief moments only, you would not trust what you heard, thinking instead I was a pesky fly bothering you. So for years this continued, our conversation never progressing."

"But I was busy, I didn't have time!"

"You didn't have time to listen to your self? Duxter, I thought by now you would be beyond making excuses. Do not dishonor me, especially with the time excuse. You always make time for things that are important. The Bellhop told you the real reason. Do you remember?"

Duxter tried to think back to his many conversations with the Bellhop, but replied that he did not recall.

"No, at the time you were not listening. Your doubts and fears were too strong. But the Bellhop told you that we do not always believe that what we want is really what we want.

"Do you remember now Duxter?"

"Vaguely, we were at the chasm, the chattering monkeys were very loud and consuming, I barely heard him at all."

"Well let me refresh your memory further. He also said that you were not yet ready to hear the message of your niggle. That is why we have not connected until now. You never believed in your Self."

Startled, Duxter jumped at what the child said. "You are my niggle? It's been you all along? Oh, I don't believe it!"

"Apparently," responded the child dryly.

"No, I mean how slow can I be? I have had that niggly feeling for years, I can't believe I wasn't listening. I didn't believe. I am sorry."

"That, Duxter, is why we have not connected until now. You never believed in your self."

Duxter sighed. "You're right. I wasn't listening. I didn't believe. I'm sorry."

The child smiled. "It's alright Duxter, few people do listen deep enough. The good thing is that now you do."

"But why don't we believe? How come it takes so long?"

"It didn't take so long. It took exactly as long as it was supposed to. This is what you meant when you concluded after talking with the master time maker that each clock develops, based on a natural flow of it's own learning. Remember, Duxter, the apprenticeship of the clocks? How some 'get it' sooner than others? You, Duxter, needed all of this journey to understand who you are and what you want."

"Hmm, I see, it's all coming together now. I did say all that. But I didn't really understand the full meaning of what I said. This really helps me to clarify some of my thoughts and learnings I have gathered."

"Well then come let me show you something that may surprise you." The child carefully lead Duxter through the fog to a cave. It was brightly lit and when Duxter walked in he noticed large murals on all four walls. At first he didn't notice the details, just how each one together illustrated a progression, someone's journey. But as he examined each one closer it dawned on him he was looking at his own progress.

"I don't believe it, it's my own travels. Hey, here I am at work talking to I Can't. And over here is the Backwards Being and the Cleaner." He smiled when he saw himself at the chasm with the Bellhop. He paused and sighed. "I seem so scared and unsure of myself."

"That time yes you were. But did you ever notice how easy it was for you to leap the chasm once you noticed your possibility?" asked the child. Duxter looked closer at the next mural.

"You're right, I do look pretty determined don't I?"

"This is important to understand so listen carefully," ordered the child. "Before you discovered your possibility you were taking the leap to get away from the state of Can't. Remember I Can't was chasing you?" Duxter laughed and nodded. "But when you saw your possibility your motivation shifted towards pursuing your possibility. This shift gave you inner power and momentum. You were no longer running away from something but moving towards a goal."

Duxter interrupted. "Would I have made it over if I hadn't seen my possibility?"

"More than likely. Many people reach their goals because they are motivated to prevent something they are afraid of from happening. But, it won't bring about the level of life mastery that you seek. Life mastery is different. The Master Time Maker discussed it. So did the chipmunk in the forest talk about the 'knowing'. Will Powers, the Bellhop and even the Professor all alluded to it. It was written in your companion book. Mastery is moving through life with a deep inner peace and understanding that you are in control. Not control over but control with all aspects of your life. It is 'Future Focus—Present Action' in everyday practice."

Duxter took the book out of his knapsack and opened it up.

"The state of being where the person's energy is focused on the way things WILL BE. He or she will make decisions and do things that move toward the future goal. This includes stopping to smell the proverbial roses at regular intervals."

Duxter nodded. The child continued. "It is the conscious and created future desired outcome or possibility with a keen awareness of what is going on in the present. This balanced perspective allows you to notice the opportunities and challenges the present provides. It also helps you to act or not to act when appropriate. You will find yourself transforming the present, putting in place the new internal habits and attitudes and external tools and supports required to reach the desired outcomes."

"Wow, with that attitude I could accomplish whatever I chose couldn't I?" Duxter exclaimed excitedly. "I think I can do it. I'm ready to get on with life."

The child smiled. Duxter hadn't noticed the child was transforming. He was growing. He was now as tall as Duxter and taking on his characteristics. "It is also time for me to get on with helping you achieve your dreams. I must go," the child said.

"But wait, how do I reach that wonderful state of being?" asked Duxter in a panic. The child was disappearing as Duxter spoke.

The child now was only a voice. "Be more aware of yourself and your surroundings. Listen to everyone you have met on this journey. But most of all look inside your knapsack. All the answers are in there. Do you remember what was written on the tag?"

Duxter's mind flashed to the description on the bag. He smiled as he recalled the tag.

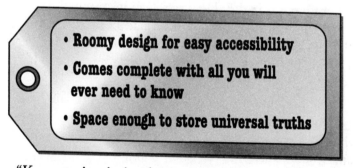

- Roomy design for easy accessibility
- Comes complete with all you will ever need to know
- Space enough to store universal truths

"Keep storing in it what you have learned. Review this learning often. Mastery will come soon enough. I will not say goodbye because I am not leaving. But again you will not see me in this or any form other than yourself, not ever again."

Leap!

Duxter's mind was reeling. He was thinking of everything and nothing. He somehow made his way out of the cave.

The shock of sunshine pushed the confusion away. Where had the fog gone, he wondered. He looked all around him, overwhelmed by the beauty and clarity he saw. He felt a shiver starting at his feet, begin to rise up his spine. The panorama was so rugged, so peaceful, so harsh. He had never seen anything like it. He was touching the hand of the Creator. He felt a higher presence, a presence he had felt as a boy but had never articulated. He was once again speechless and awestruck. The wisp of clouds seemed to be clinging to the peaks of the mountain tops, hanging on for dear life as the wind tried to pull them away. The sun was lowering in the sky, a beautiful aquamarine blue, purple with a splash of orange and yellow reflecting off the higher clouds. Stillness enveloped the earth. He could stay there all night... and he did. He lay on his back staring up at the sky. The stars were so plentiful he felt as if he could reach up and pull one down to examine it. He did. He was asleep in minutes.

In the morning, he found he had been covered with a blanket. Who had done this he did not know, but he was grateful. He folded the blanket and left it where he had been sleeping.

The breathtaking view was still there. He laughed. He had worried that somehow the view might have disappeared while he slept. He passed a sign at the elevator entrance that said—

**TO ACHIEVE YOUR PURPOSE
IS TO GET TO THE HEART
OF THE MATTER**

The elevator was waiting for him with the door open. He stepped in and descended to the ground in a flash.

There waiting for him was his possibility. It didn't say anything but it did smile and welcome Duxter into its arms. Duxter noticed that it wasn't a tall hairy creature at all, rather when Duxter looked into its eyes, he saw a limitless life and bountiful soul filled with joy and passion. He saw all that he could be and will be. He also discovered within the depths of those eyes the details of his created life. He saw how he was a writer of children's books. The thought of a more meaningful life as a writer excited him. He had no idea how long it would take or the process he would need to follow but right now that did not matter. He hugged his possibility and invited it to come along. It did so gladly. Duxter noticed how it changed shape and became small enough to fit into his knapsack. He wouldn't lose it then.

Duxter Meets An Old Friend

Sometime after that experience, which he carefully stored in his knapsack, Duxter heard a voice singing and talking. The voice was familiar to him. He checked in his knapsack for a similar experience. Yes, that was it, back at the fence, the Backward Being. It couldn't be, but there, up ahead, walking forward was the Backward Being alright. It was moving at quite a clip. That was significant. Duxter rushed up to meet it.

"What are you doing here?" exclaimed Duxter.

The Being seemed not to recognise Duxter.

"You know, back in Nowhere, at the fence, when you were stuck."

"Oh yes, that was so kind of you, to stay with me. As you can see, I have made real progress. I had the funniest experience. After you left, I met up with some rebels living in a forest and…"

Duxter and the Being talked of their experiences. It told him of his travels through ASSUMPTION, where it had made an assumption tower, to see more clearly what assumptions it had made.

"Well, I must tell you Duxter, that was a real eye opener. It is quite easy to make assumptions and you don't even need all that much information to do it. When you met me, I had made quite a beautiful assumption. My, if it hadn't been so poor, I would like to have kept it as a memento for my mantelpiece at home. But if you have good information, assumptions can disappear very quickly can't they? And so I lost it some time back."

"Just as well," Duxter replied.

"Well now, I guess you are right."

Duxter smiled. He had always felt badly, leaving the Being at the fence, but was relieved to see that it had made its own way in the world.

"I must give you something in thanks for your help," said the Being. "It is nothing really, only a quote."

Duxter was touched.

"Take only from the past what you need for the future. You will know what to take and what to leave behind."

Duxter laughed, thinking back to his own knapsack and it's rules. He put the quote in his bag. He smiled and thanked the Backward Being, "I hope we meet again... in the future." They both laughed and once again parted company.

Duxter's Dream

He was tired. It had been a very long day. He took off his knapsack and lay stretched out on the ground. Before he knew it, he was asleep.

As he slept, his knapsack started to change colour. It started to glow, getting brighter and brighter in the moonless night. The light shone all around him.

So, Duxter began to shine. Energy became part of him, he became energy.

Duxter began to dream. He dreamt of Then. The Then he was encouraged to create.

He saw his family, his wife. They were smiling at him. He felt the rebels of Can, the Bellhop, Will and the Elder, even the Master Time Maker and especially the Child. All were cheering him on to his purpose.

He saw himself open his *Companion*. He read:

When all is said and done, did you live your life on your terms?
Did you live honourably, respectfully and with purpose?

Duxter found himself projected into the future. The goal, the future possibility he wanted. He had left his career, not with fear and trepidation, but with excitement and passion. As he noticed the future, he recognized that it wasn't immediate, it was a few years from now. He saw that he was still at his job for now, but, he was setting up and organizing his change. He knew now what he had to do, whom he had to meet and what he had to learn.

He would grow into the goal over time, just as the Time Maker had suggested.

In the future, he was serving children by writing stories and telling tales. This was alright with him. He did not have to serve all mankind on a grand scale. It was important enough to know he had made a difference. He noticed that he had started telling others of his dream and noted how interested they were.

He noticed things happening, issues being resolved when they were supposed to be. In ten years, his organization had grown out of the city and into other communities. He saw hard work, he noticed stumbles but he also saw many successes. He saw commitment and focus. Perhaps his family wasn't always on side, but he knew they believed in what he was trying to accomplish.

As he traveled through his future he saw himself as an old man sitting with his grandchildren on his knee. He heard them ask, "Granddad, tell us about your knapsack." It was sitting on the floor next to his chair. By now, it was a rich chestnut brown in color. He picked it up to open it. His mind went back over his life.

"James and Clara, my children, this is the most precious gift I have ever received. It all started because…"

As Duxter started telling them, the children started to squirm in his lap. They had stopped listening.

"Go and play children, we will talk later." They jumped off his lap.

"Come play with us Grandpa," they yelled. He laughed and went with them.

Duxter Travels at Home

Duxter woke next to his wife, the alarm was ringing. He looked at the clock and smiled. He thought for a moment that he could smell... No... It was time to get going. For the first time in a very long time the "niggle" was quiet. He searched his mind for it, but it was gone. He looked over at his wife and smiled, she looked over.

"Is there something wrong?" she asked.

"No why, do I look worried?"

"No it's just, well, you seem different that's all."

"I… well…" he looked at his watch, ordinarily his morning ritual would be started, but today… "Well…" he went on to tell he about his discoveries. He explained about how the past had got in his way. He talked about how he had been going nowhere but mostly he talked about his desire to change the direction of his life. At first his wife Jenna was shocked, and upset. How could he put his family at peril like that, she asked, but Duxter expected that response and was not afraid of it. He went on to tell her that he was not going to quit his job today, rather he would work into it over time. They would both know when the time was right. Duxter looked at his watch. For the first time in a very long time he was late for work.

Duxter was late for work but what was more amazing was the fact that he forgot to read the travel section of the newspaper on his way home that evening.

Eighteen months later Duxter left his job. Well, actually he was given a severance package. He laughed when he received the letter from on high. It was signed by Smith.

His plan was to leave at the end of the year anyway so he saw the money as a wonderful gift to use to tide him over. Now he not only had money but the time he needed to put his writing career into high gear. Everything was working out just fine.

Several months later Duxter was walking down the street when he saw Smith walking towards him. Duxter noticed how Smith seemed to be walking slower. His head was down and his hands were stuffed in his pockets. Duxter actually had to stop him from walking past. Smith seemed uncomfortable to see him and it took Duxter several minutes to pry from him that he had just been let go that morning. Smith went on to say how unfair it had all been, how he had deserved more from the company than what he got. Duxter nodded in agreement and suggested they go for a coffee. Duxter wondered what he could say or do for Smith. He didn't even know if Smith wanted help but he said, reaching into his knapsack... "Look, I have this advertisement I have been saving..."

Fill Up Your Knapsack

Duxter continued his journey, always open to learning, always seeing experiences good or bad for what they were. He now realized there was no such thing as failure and that every experience had bright colorful outcomes when he was open to possibility. Sometimes he saw the learning in the experience immediately but many times it wasn't until it had remained in his knapsack for a while that he saw it for what it was. However it worked out for him, he was confident that he would create what was necessary, for whatever leap he chose to make.

Personal Reference Guide to Pursuing your Possibility

A 21 Day Program

Welcome,

I t is time now to apply the teachings to your life. You may be in the midst of pursuing a possibility or you may still be at the niggle stage, where you know something in your life needs to be improved, but you are unsure of how to proceed. Or you may be somewhere in between. In any case you will find the Personal Reference Guide to be a powerful tool.

"Possibilities," the Bellhop said, "come in many shapes and sizes," so you will find below a sampling of possibilities that clients and others have pursued. When defining the possibility you wish to pursue keep in mind the distinction the 'child' makes for Duxter between the need of the 'I' which is to play it safe and to 'look good' and the desire of the 'self' which is to achieve the highest expression of who you are. Don't sell yourself short. Go for the desires of your highest self.

Examples of Possibilities
- Strengthen personal relationships, parents, family
- Strengthen or improve marriages
- Clean up past relationships that went wrong
- Establish a new career direction
- Move to a new country to live and work
- Start a business
- Take existing business to a new level of success
- Run for public office

- Volunteer time in another country
- Be more open and honest with self and others
- Move up the corporate ladder or change companies
- Build a global company
- Write a book
- Act in the theatre
- Purchase and lead several companies to achieve financial freedom

In some cases these may seem insignificant to you but I assure you they were not so to the people who pursued them. In most cases they had been sitting on the possibility for years, letting it "niggle" at them, before they took the *Leap!* What are you waiting for?

How To Use This Section:

It is our hope that you use *Leap!* as a tool to help you go after your dreams and goals.

Below are some of the specific themes that will assist you with your Leap. You may have read the book and found others. This is fine. We recommend that you commit to starting with whichever theme you want and that you focus your attention on that theme for 21 days. To really pursue your possibility will require you to experiment with it. Try it on and practice the information. Take action, solve issues, read the appropriate pages in *Leap!* regularly and integrate the learning found on those pages. This level of attention will create the necessary "present action" you need to follow through. The Bellhop suggested that Duxter be open to learning. Please take heed of his advice.

So, here goes. Give this your best but for goodness sake have fun, because life is short.

Go to the theme that will assist you with your pursuit.

Leap!

Next to each theme are pages that provide tools, quotes, information, ideas or affirmations. Use those pages as your guide.

➡ Defining your possibility: 56, 57, 63-66, 71, 79, 121-129

➡ Breaking free of your comfort zones: 5, 19-23, 29-33, 47, 48, 50-52, 56, 58, 73, 76-80, 107-115

➡ Present Action steps to achieving your possibility: 75-80

➡ Developing Personal Power: 20-23, 30-34, 50-52, 58, 59, 71, 87-90, 96, 103-105, 121-124, 126-130

➡ Letting go of fear, worry, chattering monkeys and other unproductive thoughts: 50-52, 59, 68, 83, 92, 94-96, 101-105, 110, 113, 118

➡ Trusting yourself and your decisions: 48, 50-53, 66, 68, 76, 79, 83, 85, 92, 118

➡ Building a life mastery attitude: 20-22, 99-105, 127, 129, 130, 131

About the Author

Jonathan Creaghan is one of the most original and creative thinkers in the field of human potential and effectiveness. As an award winning personal/business coach, author and speaker, Jonathan provides powerful tools and enriching support that assist some of North America's top leaders and entrepreneurial families to fully participate in their hectic lives and focus on activities that generate true meaning and personal satisfaction.

To learn more about Jonathan's extraordinary coaching, programs and seminars visit **www.leapsafely.com**

JCg
The J. D. Creaghan Group

Leadership and *Leap!* Tools

The A-Z of Living an Extraordinary life—Meditations and Quotations on Personal Leadership

Niggles, Yabuts, Chattering Monkeys and Should Geese Quotations for engaging Personal Power—Volumes One and Two

Niggles, Yabuts, Chattering Monkeys and Should Geese Quotations for engaging Possibility—Volumes One and Two

Coaching for Leaders and Entrepreneurial Companies, the Strategic Focusing Process, Organizational Alignment Program

One on One Personal Coaching

Leadership Tools: the Pocket Companion, Inspirational Cards, Book Marks, Desk Companions and more!

Workshops and Corporate Speaking Engagements—Using Powerful Tools from *Leap!*, Jonathan leads the group on a journey of Empowerment and Self-Realization

For complete details of Jonathan's Programs and Transformation Processes, contact:

> The J.D. Creaghan Group
> 360 Queens Ave. Suite 202
> London, Ontario N6B 1X6
> 519.472.2562
> jonathan@leapsafely.com
> www.leapsafely.com

J. D. Creaghan Personal Leadership—*Designed to create outcomes you and your business know are possible!*

Tell us about your Leaps!

Real Life Stories are an inspirational source of learning and possibility. We want to learn about your experiences with your Niggle, and taking leaps—whether personal in your family or at work.

You can submit stories through our website
at www.leapsafely.com

or

The J.D. Creaghan Group
360 Queens Ave. Suite 202
London, Ontario N6B 1X6

Tel: 519 472-2562
Fax: 519 472-7030

Attn: *Leaps!*